MAINLINE
MAMA

Randy

Happy Reading ♡

MAINLINE MAMA

A MEMOIR

KEEONNA HARRIS

AMISTAD

An Imprint of HarperCollinsPublishers

This is a work of nonfiction. The events and experiences detailed herein
are all true and have been faithfully rendered as I have remembered them,
to the best of my ability. Some names have been changed in order to
protect the anonymity of various individuals involved.

HarperCollins books may be purchased for educational, business, or
sales promotional use. For information, please email the Special Markets
Department at SPsales@harpercollins.com.

FIRST EDITION

Designed by Yvonne Chan

Library of Congress Cataloging-in-Publication Data has been applied for.

ISBN 978-0-06-320569-7

24 25 26 27 28 LBC 5 4 3 2 1

*For Watts, and all the Black girls who eat Now and Laters,
play at the park, eat free lunch, and learn to swim.*

Mainline (noun)
1. A principal highway or railroad line
2. A principal vein of the circulatory system
3. Prison slang: general population (gen-pop)

Mama (noun)
1. Mother
2. Slang: wife or woman
3. Slang: term of endearment or affection

Mainline Mama (noun)
1. Black woman with relationship to prisons—through visitation or incarceration—who engages with family, children, partners, and other women
2. A population, practice, and theory of reimagining possibility from the margins
3. A particular form of precarity that also searches for joy, family, and connection in the midst of carceral state violence

Dear KeKe,

I love you.

I know you do not hear it often enough.

Today you found out you're about to be somebody's mama. Relax, girl. You're gonna make it. It's me, Keeonna. Or, I guess, I should say it's you. I'm grown now. Or, I guess, I should say we're *Grown* now.

The love that you been searching for is going to find you. You just have to be still.

I know you have big plans for yourself—stay on the honor roll, graduate high school top of the class, go to Spelman, become an obstetrician. Home feels good right now too. I know you are staying in line, as far as Mom knows. Your plans are about to change, but you will get there. You're going to break the mold and do stuff nobody in your entire family has done. There are some other lessons you have to learn first. You're good at school and going to stay good at school, but people are about to come into your life to teach you *lessons* about yourself and how to love yourself. All the bullshit you are about to encounter is going to teach you how to push on to get to everything you want.

I'm gonna need you to buckle up, because this shit is going to be a wild ride for some years. Getting caught stealing a pregnancy test from the SavOn around the block feels like the scariest thing that could ever happen. You never expect Mom to cuss you the fuck out. Your dad is going to pop up outta nowhere, for the first time in forever, to demand you get an abortion. You're going to learn all kinds of shit about the father of your child. You are going to learn that your family is greater than your bloodline. Everyone is showing you how they see you *now*, but they have no idea what you are *really* capable of doing.

It feels like you're never going to talk to Mom the same again. Someday she *will* apologize for calling you a "ho" and a "bitch." I know it sounds unbelievable, but she will. You're at the lowest point of your relationship, and someday it will be better. Today me and Mom have the relationship you always wanted. We talk all the time. I don't have to hide any part of myself from her. This bond is not going to be soon, or easy. But it will get better.

You're going to struggle, feel tired, get sick, go through bouts of depression, and feel suicidal. People you think will be there for you won't show up. You are going to feel like you're all alone. For a while. Your family and friends are around, but you're fourteen and nobody can relate to where you're at. Your family is going to switch all their visions of you from college to the workforce. Nobody is going to tell you that you're going to be good, that you're capable, that you're going to keep going. You are. Even though your granny was a teen mom and your mom was a young mom, they aren't going to give you wisdom or reassurance to guide your path. They're too busy with their own lives. They mean well, but this is life. Everybody is trying to live, and survive, and figure it out. You're going to have to figure it out yourself. Nobody is going to save you. Fall semester is going to come, but college will have to wait. You are not going to get everything you deserve when you feel like you deserve it.

You're so smart and so clever. You got more heart than any of these motherfuckers. You visited Dad and Uncle in jail, but jail is about to go from the horizon to the cloud right over your head. Prison is about to become part of all your relationships. I wish I could tell you there's an opt-out. You're going to have to deal with prison for the rest of your life.

But you'll figure shit out. Going to the prison is going to teach you how to advocate. For you, for us, for our family. And you're going to feel like things are falling apart, again. People are going to make you feel like shit. Shame is very real. Part of you is going to feel like giving up, like your soul is crawling, dragging you by your fingernails to go to work, to go to school, to just breathe.

This baby you just found out about is going to be perfect for you. It doesn't feel like it now, but he's not going to be a crier; he's not going to keep you up all night. He's going to be up, walking and talking, before you know it. Your baby is about to be an amazing child.

And even with this perfect baby, you're going to feel alone sometimes. You already feel a little alone, being the only child. But you are going to find your people. You are going to meet the best people in the places you least expect: at school, at the prison, at work. I can see your whole support network about to grow— you just won't realize it as it's happening.

I want you to know with everything ahead of you, *you* will grow. You will grow stronger. You will have great moments. You will find love. That's what we've always needed. But I know you will find it because I love you. This is the best kind of love: self-love.

So, during those times when you think you don't wanna see tomorrow, remember that I NEED YOU! I made it because *you* made it. I need you to remember that the people judging you are not half as brave, half as strong, or half as ready for the world as you are.

Love,
Keeonna

DESERT BLOOM

I run my fingers across the fabric. It's almost too perfect to take off the wire hanger. I knew this was *the* dress as soon as I saw it in the window of Lane Bryant. The saleswoman taps me on my shoulder. "Do you want to try it on?" I nod and follow her to the dressing room. "Let me know if you need anything," she says. It's long, past my knees, and white, with eyelets all over it. It ties behind my neck, leaving my back out. This dress isn't traditional by any means, not a big frou-frou beaded dress with a train or veil. The eyelets add perfect detail, like something you would wear in the country, walking barefoot in the grass. A smile comes over me because today is my day.

I'm an LA girl at heart. Even though I was raised in the city, I am obsessed with the country. Not saying I wanna be a farmer, but I resonate with the open landscapes, where you get to feel calm with all of your senses, to be mindful of everything around you—

the dew from the humidity on your skin, the sound of the water in the creek, a deep breath of clean country air. I love the shaded wraparound porches where you can sit for hours looking out at the expansive world. The country is a place I've only visited, but it's a deep part of my family history. It comes to me from stories my granny used to talk about growing up in Kilgore, Texas. Stories of her family, ten of them in a little house, everyone sharing clothes and beds. They could not afford toys, but they were content with the games they played with one another. At Christmas they would be lucky to receive a piece of fruit or a peppermint stick—something rare and sweet. They ate the same few things cooked in different ways: hot dogs on plain bread, hot dogs in beans, beans and cornbread. They didn't rely on material things to make them happy; they relied on one another.

My dress is my country, where, uninhibited by the weight of the future, I can slow down and be present. In my dress, I am finally living on my own terms, like Janie with Tea Cake in *Their Eyes Were Watching God*—laughing without having to worry about who is listening. I can take in as much happiness as my heart can hold. Instead of a veil, I wear a silk shawl big enough to cover the back of my dress and go over my shoulders. Burgundy, like the cherries I used to eat with my cousins on my granny's porch in the summer. The dress is comfortable and familiar, just like the nightgown I stole from my mom—something worn and loved for years. I touch the fabric as though it has always belonged to me. In this dress I am perfect.

I am also tired. For years I wasn't a human being but a human doing—doing tasks, taking care of whatever needed to be done. Everything was a task, checking off the list for the day to take care of the house, the kids, everybody else. Now, at twenty-five, I've been working and raising a family for a decade. This moment means I can finally breathe and be with myself.

My outfits almost never reflect my personality. Weekdays are for work: business casual, Dockers, Coach or Steve Madden flats—no makeup, nothing extra. Weekends mean only visitation-appropriate attire—nothing flashy that could draw the attention of guards. Today, though, is my day. This will be the first and only time I show up on the weekend as my authentic self: live and in color. It's my wedding day, and I'm checked in at the motel down the street from Calipatria State Prison. This isn't the bridal suite at the Four Seasons. This is a no-questions-asked truck-stop hotel where the décor hasn't changed since the seventies, which might also have been the last time they washed the sheets. For once I don't have to manage my kids; they're staying a few rooms down with my mom. But the TV isn't working, I forgot to bring my laptop and DVDs, and I'm not trying to pay the hotel rate or spend all my minutes calling people. Now it's just me waiting with my outfit for tomorrow.

The next morning I get dressed. I wear chintz lipstick, bronze like a new penny—MAC, of course—and chestnut lip liner. The rhinestones of my shimmering chandelier-cut burgundy earrings dangle and pop against my deep brown complexion. I have extensions in my short locs, so I can wear my hair up, off my neck and tucked in a French roll. My shoes—backless with a small heel-and-toe strap—are burgundy and accented with rhinestones, a perfect match with my earrings. I wait for my mom, my granny, my aunt, or my cousins to tell me how beautiful I am. I wait for someone to hold the door closed, to tell the groom not to look because it's bad luck. But it's only me in the hotel room, with the perfect outfit. I shimmer and shine.

I've never felt more beautiful. I've never felt so alone.

• • •

It's July, and I'm melting; so are my flip-flops. The bottoms leave a sticky trail wherever I place my feet. The line to the prison is always long, but today it seems even longer than usual. Calipatria State Prison is in the middle of the Southern California desert, less than fifty miles north of the US-Mexico border and almost two hundred miles southeast of Los Angeles, far from anything familiar. The prison is surrounded by alternating patches of dirt and barren fields. We are below sea level. The lower the elevation, the higher the air pressure, and the higher the air pressure, the higher the heat. You can't escape the sun out here. It feels like you're that much closer to hell.

In the middle of all this heat and dirt, cars are lined up bumper-to-bumper for miles. It's like the beginning of a disaster movie, after the evacuation notice but before everyone starts to panic. Through each car window, you can see people taking naps, changing diapers, brushing their teeth, and waiting to move even an inch. I pull past car after car until I get to Chastity's; she's saving our spot.

Chastity greets me with a glistening smile, the metal in her braces reflecting the harsh desert sun. We met through our boyfriends. We're both regular visitors, and over the past six months we've become close. We initially formed a connection around the shared circumstances of visiting our incarcerated boyfriends, and that soon evolved into a deep friendship where we truly care about each other. Chastity has developed a hard exterior over the years, but this morning her smile gives her away. She tells me and my family—my two sons, my mom, my aunie, my cousins Kawai and Ka'Nesha, my friend Shanise, and my granny—to pull our cars in front of hers.

Usually, getting in line takes all kinds of planning. Someone needs to leave their car in line early the day before. Inexperienced visitors show up early in the morning or late the night before and sleep in their cars. Chastity and our crew have a system. Someone drops off a car the day before and gets a ride back to town. This way, when we show up on visiting day, we're not at the back of a line of cars three miles long. After three hours driving from LA out to Calipatria, not having to worry about the line feels like hitting every green light with no traffic.

Still, even with the best spot, I'm impatient. I start to chew my lip to keep me occupied, using my finger to hold the inside of my cheek against my teeth and slowly scrape the inside. I keep checking the rearview mirror, popping my head out the open window to see what the holdup is. CO Davis, who passes cars through the gate every Saturday, is late. I don't want no bullshit today. Cars usually start moving at seven thirty a.m. It's seven forty-five a.m.; we're sitting still. The justice of the peace is arriving at nine a.m., and my family has to get through security. I get out and walk to my family's car to chat and ease their impatient minds, even though today they should be easing mine. I'm the bride, daughter, mother, niece, cousin, wedding planner, concierge, meal planner, and personal GPS. I need a break. Looking back at the cars stretched forever into the desert, I tell them to be ready and pay attention.

I notice the cars ahead of us start to creep toward the gate, bumper-to-bumper like a giant metal caterpillar inching forward slowly. I hurry back to my car, and as I get closer, I can see Davis, a thin, dark-skinned officer, waving for us to pull up as he waits in the booth with his aviator glasses.

"How many visiting?" he asks. There's a joviality to his tone.

I'm a regular here, so he already knows I'm with my whole family. "Me!" I say back with a laugh.

He checks my ID and gives me a visiting pass, then waves us through to the parking lot. I give everyone a once-over to make sure they're dress-code compliant. No spaghetti straps. No underwire bras. No flip-flops. No denim or chambray. No fatigues. No orange. No white T-shirts. No skirts more than two inches above the knee. No slipups today. Can't risk the guard behind the counter deciding a color is wrong, or a skirt is too short or too transparent or too formfitting. If a guard feels like it, they can hold us up or outright end a whole visit before it starts. I put on my shawl and Cinderella shoes, tossing my melted flip-flops back into the car. Everyone is ready. We walk as a family to the visitation center for Calipatria State Prison.

After everyone fills out their visitation forms and turns them in to the officer at the front desk, the next round of waiting begins. Nothing here is comfortable; everything is designed to ensure visitation is temporary. There isn't much to look at. The waiting room—full today—is filled with hard folding chairs lined up facing a giant counter. Packed behind the counter are at least eight COs and the path to the metal detector. A door leading to the bathrooms and a couple vending machines occupy the edges of the room. Any bills larger than a dollar are not allowed in the first vending machine, which sells snacks. The second vending machine sells picture ducats—the tickets are given to the porter in the visitation room so they can take Polaroids during the visit. Two dollars a ducat, one ducat per picture. The porters aren't photographers, just somebody else locked up that the prison assigned to take pictures for the day, and there are no do-overs. Luckily for us, Jason already handled the picture arrangements. All we have to do is wait for our number to be called.

Well, almost. Here's where things can go good or bad, depending on who's working behind the counter. Luckily I'm a regular and I know just about everyone—and even if I don't know the particular person working, I know how to talk my way through dress-code issues to finesse the guards and the rules. Still, today I have to get nine people through. Plus, I'm wearing a dress with no back—a violation of the dress code. I'm trying to be slick with my shawl to cover it up, but if the officer behind the security desk wants to make a big deal out of my dress, my day will grow even longer. At the desk, I take off my shoes and put my ID and money in the bins to go through the metal detector. Cash is limited to thirty dollars per adult and twenty dollars per kid, so to buy snacks, I brought a hundred fifty dollars, stacked in a neat pile of singles. Of all the dreams for my wedding, watching my whole family go through a security checkpoint was never one of them.

Prison security is a physical inspection from head to toe. The guards look through my hair, inspect every inch of my body, pat me down—all while making little comments to me, at me, or about me to one another. "Can you believe . . ." "Better you than me." "Pssh. These women." They pick me apart. And I can't say anything back. Not a peep unless they ask me a question directly. The COs have absolute authority over the security process. They can stop the whole visit because they feel like it. To see the person I love, I have to put myself at the mercy of the state.

Today I'm keeping a close eye on the eyes, faces, and body languages of the COs, trying to see what they're paying attention to. Are they pushing us all through like an assembly line? Are they chatty, wanting to talk? Are they in bad moods? I'm nervous that they might decide to make my dress an issue. I'm also watching out for my family. At any moment, an intimate and humiliating body search could become part of my wedding guests' experience.

I put my shawl in the bin, and the officer looks at me. "You know you cannot have your back out."

I put on my slickest voice. "I have this shawl, it covers my whole back, and I'll wear it the whole time, I promise."

I get lucky. We're shuffled outside into the heat to wait for the gates to the prison to open. The shooters in the towers give the all clear, and we walk through. Visiting Room C is a good five-minute walk from the gate—in 115-degree heat, on cement, in heels. The white room feels more like a storage container than a space for humans. The walls are windowless. Folded chairs are scattered and propped against the wall. The porters set them up as people check in. White posters with black text—the walls' only adornment—dictate the rules for adults and children on how to touch, how to talk: "One kiss at the beginning of visitation. One at the end." "No touching." "Hand holding is fine, but this is a family space." "Only visitors may handle money and purchase food." "Only visitors may use the microwave." "No visiting between tables." More vending machines line the walls with large "No Inmates Allowed" signs posted over every machine, and no children are allowed in the vending areas. I memorize every item they contain since I have to carry everything back to the table one item at a time. The selection is narrow—gas-station delicacies like Hot Pockets and microwave-able burgers and burritos, potato chips and pretzels. My family rarely comes to the prison, and even if they are hungry, they aren't about to eat any of that. They decide to wait while I buy food for Jason and the kids—they all have the same junk-food taste buds, and for Jason, the vending machine is an upgrade from prison food. Coming early is best; if I came later, all the good items would have been gone. Plus, with only two microwaves, coming late also means waiting in line to heat up food, wasting my limited time.

We show the officer our pass. The guard confirms the number of people in our party and shows us to our preschool-height table. We pull up the hard metal folding chairs, which are too tall for the tables, a tactic to make sure the guards can see our hands at all times. According to the pamphlets available at check-in, Calipatria's visiting rooms are meant to maintain connection between the people who live inside these walls and their loved ones on the other side. Really, though, this room is about chipping away at everyone's humanity. Everyone who enters is intimately aware that they are controlled by the state. You have to stay focused on why you're here, because it's easy to sit in this space once and never want to come back.

● ● ●

I'm filled with nerves and excitement. We're waiting on the guards to walk my groom down the prison corridor that will serve as our aisle. The door they escort Jason through is solid metal, painted white, no glass. I have no idea what's happening on the other side. Sometimes men are searched before coming into the visiting room and sent back for petty reasons, for "attempting to bring out contraband," which could be anything—something he made out of yarn, a perfume sample ripped out from a magazine, little notes to read after visiting is over. There's always a possibility that the person you're coming to see won't show up.

I'm excited until they open the door; then I am pissed. Jason's hair looks a mess. Months before the prison assigned our ceremony date, he'd decided to grow his hair out. We thought it would be long enough to be cornrowed by our wedding. It's not. It's still in that middle stage where you can't do shit with it. Too short to get braided and too long to slick back. He looks like a reject from the auditions for *American Me*: prison-blue short-sleeved shirt, CDC-issued jeans with "CDC" running up each leg in bright yellow letters, white socks, white tennis shoes. His skin is usually a very light brown, but today his face is red from nerves and drinking pruno—which, he later told me, was to help him relax. His body is covered in tattoos. Some faded, most homemade and gang tattoos he got from his friends when he was a teenager on the outside, and the rest collected over the last eleven years he's been in prison. Big block letters of his gang tattooed on his neck, a teardrop face tattoo, my granny's name on the back of his neck, and arms covered with sayings like "Trust no Bitch" and "Smile now, Cry later." To top it all off, his shiny pomade pompadour makes him look more like a used-car salesman about to sell you a busted car than a groom. I cross my arms and roll my eyes. The first words out of his mouth? "I'm sorry, I tried to get it cornrowed, but it was too short—"

I shoot back, "You shoulda shaved that shit off, then."

He tries to laugh it off and turns red. He really wanted to look nice for me; you can see the guilt on his face as his eyes go to the floor, and he avoids eye contact. His eyes get watery, and his voice starts to crack and become high-pitched like we're teenagers again. Jason is choking back the tears and telling me how pretty I look. This is our first grown-up moment; Jason has never seen me in a real dress or shoes, or with this level of makeup. Now, when it's just us and family, when none of his friends are around, he drops his guard and lets the emotions out.

We turn back to the family, and he says his hellos to everyone. We start small talk, and my anger fades as we wait for the justice of the peace. Everyone is catching up. My aunie and my younger cousin Ka'Nesha haven't seen Jason since he got locked up; he was seventeen, and I was fifteen years old. Kawai and my other bridesmaid, Shanise, have never met him in person. Luckily we all talked on the phone so often that nothing is awkward. Everything is all smiles and hellos. Phone calls let us stay up-to-date on one another's lives. Jason calls my granny collect, and she reads him Scripture. I talk to him about what's going on in family life, and I've told them all he has his own little life and community. Coffee with his friends, the new jobs he's taken on in prison, updates on his classes—first his GED, then a substance abuse counselor's certificate and Toastmasters—all the little things he does to pass the time and try to better himself. On the phone, there are no interruptions, no face-to-face policing. COs monitor calls—you're always surveilled—but on the phone, you don't have a CO watching over your shoulder. You can relax a little.

Over the phone, Jason and I get to have a full conversation. Sometimes we argue, we fight. In person, I have to keep an eye on the CO to see if they're going to get on me or him for talking too loud or step into a conversation when there's no need to. When things are good, I have to worry about a CO getting on us for hugging too long. COs don't address me directly once we're in the visiting room. They call Jason over to tell him about any rule violation and send him back to the table. They run everything, so COs could call him over for anything, from Jason touching my hand to making a comment that a CO decides is inappropriate. Getting called over by a CO is like getting called to the principal's office—everybody knows you did something wrong; it's as much about public shaming as it is about telling you what the rules are.

In the big square room with no privacy, we go to the one corner we have to ourselves. I always pictured my wedding ceremony as intimate—a few close relatives and friends. Today I have some of my family and a few friends, but we also have to invite the sixty other people in the room. All of them possibly watching and listening. The justice of the peace comes in. She's Latina, probably in her midfifties. A mix of strict Catholic grandma and school principal, she's formal, almost overdressed, with a black dress down to her ankles, black kitten heels, a fancy blouse with a broach at her neck, and a black blazer. I can tell by her attitude she doesn't want to be here any longer than she has to. She's not the prison chaplain; she's from the local town, and she just wants to go home. She starts with a very brief introduction, like in a Vegas wedding from the movies: "Today we are gathered for the union of—What's your names?" She runs through the formalities, including only what is absolutely necessary, before opening it up for Jason and me to say our vows.

I start. "I've loved you ever since I was fourteen . . ." Immediately I start crying. I'm overwhelmed by this moment, the space, the lack of privacy, the expectation that I pour out my heart in front of a crowd of people I do and don't know. In public I'm usually all business. I keep a poker face. I cry on my own time, in private. Now I'm supposed to bare my heart out to the person I love in front of a bunch of strangers. The excitement and anxiety I've felt all day now contained in this hostile prison space overflows. I catch a glimpse of Tre and Eamon out the corner of my eye, wide-eyed and with smiles I haven't seen them wear in a while. I look back at Kawai. She's always cool, but now she's crying too, and that makes me cry even more. When I don't stop, the justice of the peace turns to Jason and asks him to start reciting his vows. Even when my sobbing ends, I can't focus. I'm in full sensory overload. I have no idea what Jason said.

As soon as Jason stops talking, the justice of the peace moves to the next line of her script and asks for the presentation of the rings. You can't bring boxes into the prison, so I'm wearing both of our rings on my fingers. I slip mine off and give it to him as I take his ring off and hold it in my other hand. We exchange them.

"Okay. I pronounce you husband and wife. Kiss the bride," the justice of the peace says plainly. She's more like a justice of the peace-out. The second she stops talking, she heads for the door. We spend time as a family, with as many hugs and pictures as the prison allows, but my family doesn't want to spend their whole day in visitation. Soon enough they're ready to go, and Jason and I are ready for them to leave too. Shit, we want to have some alone time with each other. Especially because we hardly ever get a visit that is kid-free. A long, dry, and drawn-out "bye" from my mom as she is already halfway out the heavy metal door, while the rest of my family waves their goodbyes in unison, leaving Jason and me alone, or as alone as you can be in a room full of people in a prison.

The next couple of hours are our honeymoon. Pepsi and fake-butter-flavored microwave popcorn from the vending machine, talking, reflecting on how the day went, and enjoying each other's company.

The story goes that prisons are places for people who made so-called wrong choices. But Jason and I didn't choose to grow up poor. I didn't choose to be born a Black girl raised by a single mom. Jason didn't choose to get lost to the system, didn't choose to lose his mom to addiction, didn't choose to be left to family members who were supposed to look out for him but were too caught up in their own lives to really care for him. We didn't choose to be in the United States, where punishment is valued over education. Jason dropped out of school to make money and wound up in prison. I had to switch schools due to pregnancy and wound up in prison as a visitor and then as a prisoner's wife. We didn't choose to be in

California, where prisons outnumber colleges. And I didn't choose who I fell in love with.

I did have a choice about *how* to love. So I chose to control what I could. Jason's being in prison is as much about keeping me out as it is about keeping him in. Visiting him consistently for the near decade he's been inside is not only a challenge for us; it's also our challenge to the prison system. Our marriage, and my commitment to the next ten years ahead of us, is my refusal to let this place determine who I love and how I live. Getting married in a prison wasn't my dream, but I chose it because I refused to let the system dictate how I would build my family—even though I had to follow the bureaucracy, jump through all the rules of dress, guests, snacks, touching, photographs. Today is my day, and I have my wedding with the man *I* want to marry, regardless of what I had to do to have it.

"Visitation is over."

And with a brief, state-approved kiss, my wedding day ends.

Crossing back from the prison grounds into the visitor's center snaps me back to reality. The gate closes behind me, and I'm back with the guards, shooters in the towers, and the prison's ambient noise.

I walk alone on pavement, back through the reception area, to the parking lot, farther and farther from the visiting room. Now I'm smiling and proud: I had my wedding and my day, and nobody stopped me. Chastity and my homegirls visiting their loved ones on other yards meet me in the parking lot. We pile into my rental minivan to go to Golden Corral for my reception.

Tomorrow I do it all over again. This time no dress. No shiny shoes. No makeup. No family. Just me, Jason, and Calipatria State Prison.

AIN'TS

In 1994 I was fourteen, in junior high, and me and Autumn was thick as thieves. She was a year older, but in accordance with the best friend code, she was determined that I meet her boyfriend's best friend, Jason, so we could hook up—or really, so she could get some alone time with her man. When we finally met, I was not impressed. Jason had too many ain'ts.

1. Ain't got no car
2. Ain't in school
3. Ain't Black
4. Ain't a Crip
5. Ain't tall
6. Ain't ballin'

Jason wasn't grown and mature in the ways I thought I deserved. Besides, he was everything I wasn't used to. I come from a Black,

Crip neighborhood, and even though I wasn't personally involved in any gang activity, where you're from defines your affiliation. Jason is Mexican, and a Blood covered in tattoos. He's proud of it too. If he was going into a Crip neighborhood, he was coming through with a tank top on to show off his tattoos, just inviting trouble. He couldn't come by where I stayed, and I couldn't go to certain places with him.

But after a few weekends, Jason started to grow on me. He didn't talk much, and he always had this mean look on his face. He had these long eyelashes and these beautiful hazel eyes that said more than he could with words. There was a sadness in those eyes. Both of his parents were dead, and he'd dropped out of high school a couple years earlier. At sixteen he was a gang member and lived in a motel, then a dope house. He came off as a mean little asshole, acting like a bully, overly aggressive, in people's faces with smart-ass comments. And he made sure people knew he was carrying a gun.

Even though I wasn't into him at first, Jason was drawn to me. His attention made me feel special—safe, wanted, loved, seen, and valued; a priority. He made me feel like nothing bad could happen to me, to us. He was the first one to throw a punch when people acted aggressive, quick to flash his gun at anyone who was rude to me because it would end any argument before it even started. He wanted me to keep separate from his life on the streets. One time I showed up on his block, and we got into a big argument because he knew it wasn't safe for me to be there and wanted me to go home. That's when I knew he was looking out for me, no matter what.

Jason and I came from places that were different but so alike. His mom was a drug addict and wasn't there for him; his dad had died when he was a little kid. My mom worked nights as a nurse, and she'd wake up right as I was getting ready for bed and walk in the door right as I was about to walk to catch the bus to school; my dad bounced when I was young. We both respected our mothers above everything. We prioritized loyalty. We both cared so deeply about family and craved that family connection. Everything that we were missing—family, love, acceptance of who we were as we were—we found in each other. We fell in love, and we held on for dear life. That was the beginning.

• • •

Everything changed when I started ninth grade. Before that year, I had balanced good grades and doing what my mom said with going to parties, drinking, talking to boys. At fourteen, I thought I was so mature, flirting and acting grown. I would get into cars with boys who didn't have a license but knew how to drive, meet up with friends in the next city over, drink at somebody's house when their parents weren't around, and come back home like nothing had happened. I didn't ask permission. I was set on going to Spelman and becoming an obstetrician. My grades were still good, and my mom worked. So if I didn't send up any red flags, I could get away with anything. Still, I never got physical with anybody. I wasn't even allowed to have a boyfriend. Playing grown meant playing a tease to get the attention and money I desired. I played the most dangerous game of flirt with grown men. I knew what they wanted with me, with my body, but I also knew what I wanted. And I knew what I had to do to get what I wanted without giving up anything. I went as close to the line as possible without touching. When they realized I wasn't going there, most gave up and ignored me. I couldn't ask my mom for stuff, but I liked buying my own food, so I could get Mrs. Fields cookies or Hot Dog on a Stick without having to ask. I played double Dutch with life; the rope whirled around me, and I always jumped out the way before I got caught up.

When I met Jason, I still wasn't giving it up, but Jason showed up anyway. He stayed around in ways that nobody in my life had done up to that point—not my mom, definitely not my dad. One night, after a few weeks of hanging out, Jason asked me to be his official girlfriend. I was at Autumn's house, where I spent every weekend. Autumn's house was my safe place. At her house I felt seen and free, which was something I no longer had at home. Up until this time in my life, no matter if the adults in my life showed up or not, my cousin Kawai always did. But during my seventh-grade year, she moved out of the apartment with me and my mom, and back in with her parents. If that wasn't bad enough, her parents bought a house in LA, which was at least a thirty-five-minute drive from us, and she started playing basketball, which took over her whole damn life. We barely saw each other anymore. With Kawai and I being separated, I was so grateful that God blessed me with Autumn. I was an only child, and Autumn was like an only child. She has, like, five other siblings who are old enough to actually be her mother; she's one of those accident babies. Autumn's mom was in her late fifties when we were in junior high, and she was a custodian at the high school. That meant that on Friday, when she came home, it was a simple recipe: she would shower, grab a few Budweisers from the fridge, grab her Virginia Slims off the counter, and tell us to be good, and then she would disappear down the corridor. She was tired, resting, and trusted us to behave like we was supposed to. She was a rare parent that respected our privacy and let us be ourselves in her house. As a kid I thought she was the cool parent, but looking back as an adult and parent I know she was tired from manual labor and trying to use her weekend to get some rest. It was easier to trust us. At Autumn's house I felt free again. Autumn and me and all the other young folks in the apartment complex got to be ourselves, minus the surveillance of adults.

One weekend Autumn and I were sitting on the couch, watching music videos on BET, our favorite channel, rappin' along to "One More Chance" by Biggie Smalls. There was a knock on the door. Autumn looked out the peephole: it was our homeboy Sam, who used to live upstairs with his parents and four other siblings until they got evicted. Funny thing: out of the year or so they lived upstairs, I never met his parents; they were always working. Both had two jobs, with four kids in a two-bedroom, but they were always away, working. With all the adults out working or up to something else, we were all like adults. Me, Autumn, and Sam would regularly kick it, talk shit, drink, smoke, and, if we were really bored, flirt with one another. Out of all his siblings, Sam was the coolest. Everyone knew he had a little crush on me, but I wasn't feeling him like that. He was about five years older than us, which made him grown for real; he was eighteen but still came to hang with us. Sam was just a good, regular boy. Even with his parents each working two jobs, they were barely getting by. Sam usually had some clean, saggy jeans, and a clean white tank top. Nothing flashy, nothing nice, but not messy. He seemed like he was one of the few dudes in the apartment complex who wasn't a smoker or a dealer. The thing that made Sam so cool to me was that he never pressed me; it's like he had a code. Unlike the other boys and men who came around, he cared that I was underage and never pursued me.

That night, when Sam came over, Autumn flung the door open. We all sat on the couch, catching up on the latest gossip of the

Woods apartment complex and him giving us a rundown of where he lived now and what his family was up to. Sam was dressed nicer than usual, but for him that just meant some jeans that actually fit and a plain, regular T-shirt. Then there was another knock. Autumn and I locked eyes. She got up, and it was her boyfriend, Rodrick. We were shittin' bricks! We wasn't doing anything wrong, but, shit, it's all about code. No matter what the situation, your dude coming over and another nigga sitting on the couch was not a good look. She was not trying to hear her nigga mouth, but more importantly, I didn't want Rodrick going back and saying shit to Jason. I already knew how this type of situation worked out—shit, I'd been watching my granny, mama, and aunie and their relationships with men for years. And it doesn't take a rocket scientist to come to figure out that male "friends" are not allowed when you're in any type of romantic relationship with a boy or man, unless you're trying to start shit. I knew this would not end well. I could feel the knots forming in my stomach.

"Shit," Autumn said under her breath.

"Who is it?" I said in a whisper.

"Rodrick."

"Don't open the door—"

Before the words flew out my mouth, she was already opening it. As Rodrick stepped into the doorway, I saw someone following right behind him. Jason pushed Rodrick aside and set his eyes directly on Sam. Autumn was still standing by the door; I was sitting on the love seat, and Sam was sitting on the other couch. We all were silent. I could tell that Sam was scared, because his eyes stayed fixed on the carpet, and he kept brushing the nonexistent lint or whatever off his jeans. Jason was now quietly hovering over Sam. Jason took off his jacket and handed it to his friend. Once the jacket was off, you could see the butt of a gun sticking out the front of Jason's khakis, and the tattoos on both arms. Jason was a short, stocky gang member with a reputation in the complex, because that was where he sold drugs. Everybody knew who he was, so Jason's version of peacocking didn't need flare or feathers, just a cold stare, showing his tattoos. When Jason gets aggressive, he doesn't get loud; he gets quiet, calm, and pointed. Sam knew not to say anything while Jason announced himself. "I'm Macc. Where you from? I know yo brother is a Crip. It's Blood on mines. What's up?"

Before Sam could think to talk, Jason started drilling Sam with more questions: "Who are you? Who are you here to see? Didn't you used to like Keeonna?" I was scared and embarrassed. Scared because I didn't want any harm to come to Sam, and embarrassed because I always carried myself as tough and confident, and, in that moment, I was out of my normal character. Shortly after his interrogation, Sam quickly made his exit. My heart was racing like I had just watched them fight, but there was no commotion, just calm intimidation. Autumn's mom didn't even have to yell out the room to see what was going on. Rodrick and Jason coming over wouldn't have changed anything either. Even though they were dealers and gang members, Autumn's mom was cool with them. Jason and Rodrick knew the game—they were clearly up to no good around the apartment—but they would give her a hundred dollars every now and then for groceries. They were buying her peace.

Jason sat next to me on the couch. He reached into my backpack and grabbed my notebook and a pen. He started to write something on the front of my notebook; when he handed it to me, it read "Jason loves KeKe." Now we were official. I saw Jason every weekend, and when I went to Autumn's house, Jason would be there too. I would catch the bus after school and Jason would know to come by, and the four of us would kick it for the weekend. Watching the latest videos on BET. Talking. Later, on Friday nights, Jason and Rodrick would go to sell dope but come back through later in the night to kick it or sleep over. No sex, no messing around: they would sleep on the couches, me and Autumn would go sleep in her bedroom, and they would let themselves out early in the morning to get back to work. I thought Jason's courtship was sweet. He was always considerate of me and didn't overstep my boundaries.

I misread his possessiveness as passion. I thought Jason was what I needed. I thought I knew what I was doing. I thought I was playing men to get the things I wanted, but Jason gave me something nobody else could and something I didn't know I wanted. I wanted to be wanted. I wanted someone who would show up for me. I needed someone who would be there. Behind all the toughness, in our relationships—me and Jason, Autumn and Rodrick—we were typical teenagers, sitting around, kickin' it on the weekends together. We were playing like adults without supervision, but we took that freedom to just be kids and spend time together. For Rodrick and Jason, Autumn's was a safe haven too, a short escape from the outside of drugs and gangbanging. I wasn't allowed to have boyfriends and I lived in a whole different city, so nobody was coming to my house, and Jason didn't go to my school. So we saw each other on the weekends at Autumn's. We didn't go out—no dinners, no movies, no cars. Just stayin' in at Autumn's house, in front of the TV or people-watching from the balcony. We didn't even talk during the week because, like I said, I wasn't supposed to have no boyfriend, so we were only together on the weekends. For months we were a real teen couple, holding hands, kissing, watching TV, kickin' it. Barely even PG-13.

One weekend we were all kickin' it again like usual. Autumn and Rodrick decided to have sex, and I got assigned to play look-out. We all started out in the living room, but in Autumn's house there was a long hall from the living room to the bedrooms, and doors to every room in the hallway. Autumn and Rodrick had a whole little pallet set up in the kitchen, laid out on blankets, but me and Jason were staying in the living room to listen for Autumn's mom and knock on her door if there was a problem. Jason and I had time to ourselves, still just sitting and enjoying each other's company. We started kissing, and the kissing got heavier, and quickly I realized Jason thought we were about to have sex. I knew what sex was, and pregnancy; my mom had given me the talk years ago. But I figured pregnancy was something that happened to people who had sex a lot. I also knew Jason loved me; I knew he cared for me and always showed up. I figured, *Why not?* I could show him that I loved him too. This was my first time, and our first time together, but it wasn't his first.

We were supposed to be playing lookout, but Autumn's mom was the tiny version of Dionne Warwick: short like Autumn, thin as a rail, dainty, and always puffing on Virginia Slims, but she was mostly just in her room drinking Budweiser and watching TV. She usually just took a few beers to the room and stuck to herself for the night. The smart move woulda been for Autumn and Rodrick to go to her room and lock the door, but we were probably more worried about getting in trouble for the locked door. I take ownership, because I wasn't paying attention. Autumn's mom was so little and I was so occupied, nobody heard when she came out the room, went to the kitchen, and caught Autumn and Rodrick. I got caught slippin', but me and Jason didn't get seen. So much for lookout. Everything went quiet at Autumn's house for a while. It didn't dawn on me till more than a month later that I had missed my period. That's when I found out I was pregnant with my son Tre. Off the first time having sex.

No more double Dutch. Now I *had* to go to college for me, *and* Tre, *and* Jason. I had wanted to go to college ever since I saw Dr. Huxtable on *The Cosby Show*, but what I really wanted was to be loved and seen as a person. Not somebody who was just doing stuff for somebody else. Somebody to be used. Or somebody to be ignored. I knew my mom loved me, but she was working two jobs, so I didn't get to see her love. To Jason, college was something on TV. He was homeless, a high school dropout, a gang member, and a drug dealer. He lived in *New Jack City*, not *A Different World*. But he liked that I had dreams. He always said I was good. He saw me going to school, getting good grades; he was always supportive of me going to school. He didn't want me ditching or jeopardizing anything. He saw himself as part of my life forever; he didn't think about how college could mean me leaving him behind. For Jason it was about keeping me on my path and supporting my dreams. He wasn't thinking about himself. That was part of the problem. Jason tried to make quick money on the streets to make up for everything he never had. He stayed out all night selling dope, stealing cars. Jason didn't have the words to tell me he cared—nobody ever taught him—so he showed me with money that he was all in.

COLLECT CALL

Jason was my mom's worst nightmare—a seventeen-year-old dealer who got her daughter pregnant, derailing my life and her dreams for me. He encapsulated all the problems my dad had caused for her, times a thousand. I knew Jason sold dope, but to me that was normal. I grew up in Watts in the eighties. Some people got money from dope, and some spent their money on dope. My dad was a dope boy. It wasn't nothing new to me.

I didn't understand how deep in the game Jason was. He didn't spend his drug money on flashy shoes or clothes or jewelry. He put his money back into being a gang member. I didn't see how his gang-bangin' was more than just on the surface, until about two months before our baby was born. My stepdad, Bert, tried to convince Jason to get a legit job to provide for me and the baby, but that wasn't possible. Bert used to be in the streets—not at the level of Jason or my dad, but he was street-smart, gambled, knew people who could get things, and had a real day job working at NAPA. My mom saw me as Keeonna, the little kindergarten valedictorian who kept things clean. Me and Bert used to listen to Ice Cube together. He saw me for me, and he saw Jason for who he was and who he could be. Jason explained to Bert—even before he got the nerve and explained to me—that he was on the run from the police because of his gang activity. Bert was ready to get him a fake ID and a job at NAPA; he tried to convince Jason to come stay with us and put his whole life on a different path. Bert had been with my mom since I was in fourth grade, and they got married when I was in seventh grade. Bert knew my mom was not going to accept Jason as he was, but Bert offered to turn him into somebody respectable that my mom could maybe accept. Jason wasn't interested. Jason thought he could figure it out himself. Right before our son was born, I asked Jason what he wanted to do with his life. He wanted to be "the meanest gang member." Dealing drugs wasn't just about money or flash, like it was for my dad. Jason wanted the reputation, the power, and the respect he thought came from fear. If people are scared of you, that's the ultimate currency on the streets. He succeeded.

The money was one thing; making money selling drugs was just a thing people did. He was really with the shenanigans—gangbangin', flashing his weapon just because. Power and control on the streets came from fear of violence, which had to be physical and shown in actions. I wasn't worried about all that. I was a tough girl, I could take care of myself, but Jason knew that he had a target on his back, so we never went anywhere in public. I felt safe from harm, because he knew not to put me in harm's way. I didn't start to worry until I was pregnant. Jason showed me he loved me with his actions. He didn't know how to talk about feelings, with me or anyone.

After I found out I was pregnant, we didn't really talk. There was a weird space of trying to figure out the new normal. Our whole shit got blown up. Once my mom found out, and once she realized I wasn't the girl she thought I was, me and Jason had to figure out new ways of communicating. We didn't see each other for a while. I was able to page him and have quick calls from the pay phone around the corner. I had to call everybody from that phone since my mom took away all my phone privileges. I wasn't just grounded; she took all the phones out of the house and locked them up in her room. Good thing nothing happened when she wasn't home. I would page Jason with our special code, and he'd call the pay phone back. My mom was clear: no more Autumn's house, no more Jason, no more going out. Just home and school. They didn't want me at my old high school when I was pregnant. I wasn't kicked out, but I had a lot of teachers ask me, "Wouldn't you be happier at a place with other girls like you?" I got the message. I found a new school that would allow me to attend during and after the pregnancy, with a day care center to watch babies while school was in session. And it was only a block from my house. It was magical, like the school was just waiting for me the whole time. All the moms with kids had an elective to work in the day care center, helping with the kids. The school was there for us to all help one another.

Once I started going to the new school, things were smooth. Two weeks in I got called to the front office. The front office meant concern, so I got up to the front, and there was Jason. He wanted the key to my house so he could be waiting for me. He didn't have a car or anywhere else to go, so I gave him the key so he could shower. He always showed up when he could get a ride from the woman—we called her only the taxi lady—who drove Jason around in exchange for drugs. She would really drive him from West Covina to Glendora, a good twenty-minute drive. After that first surprise, Jason and I figured out how to spend time together: he would show up to walk me home every other day. Jason waited for me by the schoolhouse gate; it wasn't crowded and we got out early, so he was easy to spot. We would walk, talk, and he would buy me food because, hello, I was pregnant. I needed snacks. There was a mom-and-pop diner around the corner called B&J, where we would share a plate of chili-cheese fries. I was addicted because I was a hungry pregnant girl, and he loved the fries too but got to play supportive and eat along with me. That's when we would catch up; I got to fill him in on doctor's appointments, new developments in my life, and he would tell me his wild stories of the streets.

If it was the beginning of the month, he'd be exhausted. First of the month meant all the smokers got their checks, so he'd be all red-eyed and tired from being out all night selling dope. He would take a shower and quick nap at my house while my mom wasn't home, because that was the only place he felt safe. My house was like the spa to him. He got a long shower, nice lotion, everything he didn't have. He could leave his dirty clothes over there, and I would wash them, but while he slept, I could sit next to him in my bed and watch TV in my room. I got caught up on Richard Bey and Jenny Jones, with one eye on the clock to make sure we didn't get too comfortable and I could get him out of my room and out of the house before my mom or stepdad got home. Before he'd leave I'd always make him a quick egg sandwich. He liked the way my eggs tasted, and he loved the trivial homemade food, because if he wasn't at my house, he was at a Motel 6 or dope house, where he'd have to be on guard.

His reality was on the street, where communication is all about presentation—you say what you mean and how you're feeling with an iron fist, and there's no room to be emotional. Jason on the streets was every gangster-movie stereotype. He didn't talk; he acted. No yelling, no arguing. A miscommunication wasn't an argument; it was a fight waiting to happen. But when he came to my house for those few hours, he was a cuddler. He'd barely slap hands or show love to his friends on the streets. When we were sitting in bed, he wanted to be close and touch. Some of the walks home he would show up with presents to show me he cared. Sometimes little stuff, like chili-cheese fries just the way I liked, a Taco Supreme from Taco Bell, some clothes for the baby from the new Walmart down the street. Contributing made him feel good, and he knew how to show up with things I wanted or needed.

One weekend my mom and stepdad went to Vegas, which meant Jason came over for us to spend time. He was supposed to come over on Friday, but he was out robbing houses, so he didn't come over till Saturday. I was expecting something ordinary, but when he pulled out a ring, all I could think about was how ugly it was. A small pearl-cluster ring with some diamonds on the side. Something my granny would wear to church, not something I would ever wear on my finger. It was giving sixty-five-and-up motherboard at the church, elder show-me-some-respect, not fifteen-year-old shop-at-the-Sanrio-store Keeonna. He saw it as a promise ring, he always said we would get married, and he came across it during his thieving. He usually sold off everything, but he thought it was pretty, so he wanted to give it to me to let me know that he had plans for us to be together in our future. This was a seventeen-year-old with visions of the future. I still thought the ring was so ugly, but he was so sweet, he melted my heart. I didn't tell him how ugly it was to hurt his feelings, but I took it and appreciated him for it. So I stashed it in my lavender Caboodles jewelry box. Even if I had liked it, my mom bought all my jewelry, so if she saw me wearing it, it was over. A few years later I finally took it out—to pawn it. I had to pay for all the phone calls from Jason once he was in jail.

Our relationship was the only place I heard Jason try to talk about feelings. Words of love and compassion that he reserved for only me. But since he saved those words for me, he knew he couldn't get what he wanted if he held his words back. We were both looking for the same kind of compassion and respect that we thought we could find only in each other. We were drawn to each other like magnets; it seemed natural and connected, even though I now see I was drawn to what he used to repel others. Outwardly we were opposites. I was a good, clean, going-to-school girl, on track for college and a big future, but I could also hang in the streets as a tough LA girl, but not a square. He was harsh and direct in the streets, all tough, no need to talk, but had a sweetness and attentiveness to him that he only shared with me. He showed up, constantly and consistently. He didn't just say he cared and walked away. I knew my mom loved me; she showed it by being out, working hard, paying the bills, and keeping the house together. I knew it, but as a teenager I was looking for show-and-tell. I had seen dope boys my whole life, so that didn't do anything else extra for me. I knew he was a raggedy, homeless, ashy boy. The dope dealers I was used to were flashy, clean, and put together. I wouldn't have paid no mind to Jason, but he was so sweet to me. Selling drugs was so normalized, there was no bad-boy attraction once Jason showed me what was behind the tough gangster image. Jason struggled to say it, but he knew how to show he cared by showing up physically, being there, bringing gifts, saying kind words. The masks we wore for everyone else in our lives we got to take off with each other, and that felt special and real. Sharing vulnerability was a sincere form of love I hadn't seen from anyone else, so I just accepted all the other parts of Jason too—the violence to others, the gangbanging, the slick mouth in conversations. I knew people who had gone to jail, that the police could grab him, and that he could get locked up. Just like the pregnancy, I thought that getting killed or going to prison was something that happened, and it wouldn't happen to Jason. During the pregnancy, I knew I could raise this baby, and I imagined us doing it together, even with Jason being on the streets. Once the baby was born, it fully set in that he could be locked up or killed. I would lose him, and everyone would say shit about me being stupid for being with him or tell me how I was in over my head. All of this started a burning nausea in my stomach, but I pushed it down. I convinced myself things wouldn't be that bad. We would get married and be okay.

About eight months after Tre was born, my mom and stepdad were out of town for the weekend in Vegas again. By the time I got out of school, my mom and stepdad were already off to Vegas, so I hurried home, pushing Tre in the stroller to get to the house. The house stayed clean. It always smelled like Pine-Sol, and that was the way my mom liked it. Keeping everything nice and clean made up for anything that wasn't top-of-the-line brand-new. After I got into our little town-house apartment, I went into the garage and left the stroller and carried my baby upstairs. He loved to play with the measuring cups and pots and pans, so I set him up on the nice clean floor to keep him distracted. I took out the ground beef to thaw and checked all my ingredients to make sure we didn't have to go back out in the stroller to the corner store to get any extra supplies. I paged Jason before I started cooking because I wanted to make sure he was going to be there before I got my elaborate feast together. He called back to tell me he would be here around eight. Bet, that meant we could eat, watch TGIF, movies, and just be together without having to be rushed or sneak around. I prepared our grown-up meal—extra-cheesy cheeseburger Hamburger Helper and Jiffy corn bread. A feast.

Once I finished cooking, I fed Tre his baby food while he was sitting on the floor. We didn't have a high chair, but the floors stayed so clean, I could just sit with him on the floor with a towel to clean up any messes. He was always such a good eater, I didn't have to barely clean up. Once he was fed and washed up, I put him down for the night around eight. Now I was done with all my responsibilities and my evening was clear, so me and Jason could just spend time together.

I posted up on my mom's good couch, laughing at Steve Urkel on TV, and I lost track of time. I was pissed because Jason was late again, so I was just going to go ahead and eat without him. I start paging him so he could at least check in, and I started eating Hamburger Helper, waiting for Jason. He was supposed to come at eight. Suddenly the whole TGIF lineup was almost over, the credits rolled on *Hangin' with Mr. Cooper*, and he still wasn't there. We never got to kick it like this—just the three of us, with the house to ourselves. I knew Jason wasn't passing up a rare family moment. The same feeling had bubbled up when I realized my dad wasn't going to be in my life anymore. I wasn't mad. I got calm; everything became clear and simple. By that point in my life, I was used to being let down by men. No anxiety, no fear, no nerves. A big wave of nothing washed over me. Usually, I'd page Jason, then call his friends' houses looking for him. But this time I didn't. I knew he wasn't coming. I went up to my room and turned on the TV to go to bed.

My phone rang before the sun was up. Too early to be anything good.

"You have a collect call from . . . Jason."

Jason told me he was in jail. And he wasn't getting out tomorrow, or anytime soon. On the way to my house, Jason had stopped at Jack in the Box. He saw some niggas slipping and decided to take their car. In his mind he was going to jack the car, sell it for money, and give me the money for Tre's clothes and diapers. He was arrested for attempted carjacking.

He had mentioned a couple months prior that he was on the run because he shot somebody. He hadn't given me the details at the time, but I knew what was up. He was a gang member. Shootings happened. I hadn't even thought to ask for details, because if there was a shooting and he wasn't hurt, that was just another day in the life. That's a separate issue, apples and oranges. I didn't ask questions. That was a different world from us together in our family unit; him being a gang member on the streets was just another part of him. He was a complex person, and to keep it real, I wanted me and Jason and the baby to be together, and I hoped Jason would be around, but my dad was a whole drug dealer who had been to jail. There was nothing I hadn't heard or seen or thought of before. Tre was still a baby; I was trying to be supportive of Jason getting his life together. I found out months later that while Jason was on the run, my stepdad, Bert, tried to get Jason a fake ID and a job at the auto store where he worked, even inviting him to come stay with us. Bert never told me about it, but he was working behind the scenes trying to get me and Jason and Tre on the right path as a family. Bert never kept me in the loop because he didn't want to seem like it was us against my mom; he would talk to Jason and talk to my mom and leave me out of it. I was thinking of a future where we could get married and have a family life together. I was still naïve to the real criminal justice system. I saw people go to jail, but they came home. People were taking penitentiary chances thinking that a chance at losing five years was an even trade for the flashy life. I knew the system was racist, I knew people were getting caught up by police in cruisers and tanks, I saw people shooting each other and going to prison for murder. I didn't understand three strikes, gang enhancements, and mandatory minimums. I had seen people go to jail, but I was only just starting to see people get swept off the streets in piles, taking an entire generation of boys into prison. I figured Jason on the run meant he could get caught, but if he did, he wouldn't be gone for too long.

I never saw any courtrooms for any of Jason's trial. He didn't want me there and my mom didn't want me there, so I couldn't even sneak over to the courthouse. I was sixteen, with no car and a whole baby. The trial took almost a year. During that time I was trying to finish high school with a baby. I saw Jason maybe four or five times in the whole year, when my granny would take me to the downtown LA jail to go visit him. At this time in LA, the only jail was the Men's Central Jail. Waiting in line for hours for a fifteen-minute glass call. First you stood in a long line that was on a cement ramp into the visiting room, on the outside of the building. Visiting hours were from two to five, so you had to get in line and wait. Nothing but a cement ramp and a metal rail that curled around the entire building. It was like in elementary school when the playground had the one metal bar that came out the ground for kids to climb and swing around, but nobody here was playing. You just had to stand, lean, or sit on the ground. At the time, the only things downtown were skyscrapers for the big businesses and courts. Visiting was right by Receiving and Release, so it was only people getting out of jail and people sleeping on the streets, while everybody else was in the skyscrapers at work or in court. I tried to get there right at two, because then Granny could come with me and we could get home before traffic and make dinner. I was a minor without a car; I needed her to drive and be there with me through the whole process. My mom for sure wasn't going to take me.

After an hour of waiting, at least, you got to the front, and the officer handed you a visiting pass. I filled it out for me and my granny, because I didn't need her putting anything on there that would mess it up. And by this time, Jason was eighteen and I was sixteen, so I couldn't walk in the door and say I was his girlfriend, because I wasn't trying to complicate anything. I'd just tell them I was his cousin bringing his baby to visit him, if they wanted to know why me and my granny, who were both very clearly, visibly Black, with this clearly light-skinned baby, were coming to visit this boy named Jason Espinoza.

Once we got in, we walked down a long row of little steel booths and small steel privacy walls, with corded phones bolted to the wall. Each booth was barely big enough for one person, but they let up to two people sit at a booth to visit. Everything in the call room was steel, bolted to the floor, and musty. It was nasty, had never been upgraded, paint chipping off the walls showing more steel underneath. The only thing not stuck to the ground or the wall was the standard-issue hard plastic chairs that were in every government office of the nineties, easily wiped and stacked, durable but easily replaceable. Me and Granny walked down the row of little booths to get to our assigned area, and it was a full tour of everybody at the jail. Before the visitors got in, folks waiting for visits were already on the other side just sitting. Some were talking to themselves; some had been on the streets forever, looking disheveled and dirty; some looked like regular folks who might have lived down the street; some looked like they worked in one of the skyscrapers down the block. When we got to our assigned seat, I made sure to clean the phone because if the person who used it last had bad breath, I didn't want to be smelling it the whole time we were talking.

We only had fifteen minutes for our visit, so there was no time to talk about anything real, just the niceties. "Hi, how you doing, how's the baby, how are you." He couldn't talk about anything real because the guards were there, and he didn't want anyone listening to anything. This jail was also gangbangin' central, different modules for Bloods and Crips. So when I saw Jason, I saw bruises on his knuckles, a cut on his lip, a bruise on his face. He had come into jail swinging, letting people know where he was from and who he was with from the jump. Seeing his face let me know immediately how things were going for him. Even though Tre was a baby, it hurt my heart to have him see his dad bruised up like this, but there was no other way for Tre to see his dad. I knew and Jason knew that this was the only way to talk to or see each other at the time. I had to put a million things in motion for fifteen minutes of time. It seemed pointless to talk Granny into driving me down there, give her gas money, pay for parking, sit through the hour or more of waiting to say "Hi, how you doing" for fifteen minutes, and go home. Jason didn't want me coming to court or to the jail that much anyway. I think deep down he didn't want me hearing everything he had done or seeing him locked up.

My mom didn't want me seeing Jason at all. Far as she was concerned, he was the one who blew up my life. I was still trying to prove to my mom that nothing had changed from the image she had of me before I got pregnant. I was still the same girl who was valedictorian of her kindergarten class, staying in school, getting good grades, and on my way to college. The only thing that changed was the baby, and I was determined to show her that didn't change anything. My mom only met Jason twice before he went to jail, and I found out about the other encounters secondhand.

My mom and Jason first met over the phone, right after she found out I was pregnant. I hadn't even told my mom anything about Jason; she got his information from Autumn. Jason didn't even know I was pregnant yet. My mom got Jason's information and paged him just to get him to call so she could cuss him out. Jason handled it *horribly* by talking back to her. I didn't even find out they had talked until a few days later.

The second time my mom met Jason was in person, after she brought me home from the hospital with Tre. He called the house to ask my mom's permission to come visit me and the baby. She said yeah, no conditions, no explanations, just permission. Jason had come to visit me and the baby, but he brought flowers for me and my mom. He was doing his best to play the nice, respectable young man. Some adult had obviously told him to do it, because the whole time we were together, he brought me things to show me he cared, but never once had he brought me flowers. Out of character, but it showed, at least to me, that he was trying hard to impress. When he got there, my mom answered the door; she waved him over to the couch, telling him to sit down without saying a word. I was on the stairs of our little house trying to peek around and see, but she waved me back upstairs. She came back upstairs and finally spoke. "This ain't no good-time party, y'all not together, he gonna sit down there and visit his baby, and you gonna stay your little silly ass upstairs." I of course had nothing to say; she took the baby down to the living room to visit. From my room I could hear him talking to the baby, obviously uncomfortable because he was a seventeen-year-old gangbanger who didn't talk to people, let alone kids, let alone babies. Add on to the fact that my mom kept such a clean house, our living room didn't even look lived-in. It looked crisp and clean like a *Fingerhut* catalogue, but more unwelcoming. Pretty like a showroom, but designed like a space where people weren't supposed to be. My mom put in a lot of work to keep it looking brand-new. It was a room to be looked at, not lived in.

This was the second time Jason and my mom met, but the first time he was navigating my family without me guiding him. I was usually taking his side and trying to explain everything to my mom, but even though we had a baby together and Jason promised to help out, by that point Jason and I were not planning on being together. When I was seven or eight months pregnant, we had already drifted apart. I was busy focused on my baby and going to school; Jason was busy back in the streets. When Tre was about to be born, I expected him to slow his roll in the streets and ease up, but from what I saw, he was getting worse. Visits got less frequent because he was always out looking for the next come-up. Out selling dope, breaking into houses to sell shit, and stacking money. Our time together was dwindling as he got deeper into the streets. He would explain to me later he thought he was being helpful. For him, this was the first time he felt like he had a purpose and was doing everything in his power to contribute. He didn't have a regular job, so he was looking for money to support Tre. For me, it was too much to handle. It was a very short breakup—we were back together in a couple months—but I was dealing with a lot at the time, and I had just pushed a whole baby out of my body a few days before, and we weren't together.

Quickly into Jason's downstairs visit, Tre got hungry, so my mom allowed him to come upstairs into my room while I fed the baby, of course with the door open. I was sitting on the right side of the bed, facing the window and the stereo, feeding the baby, while

Jason was sitting on the opposite side of the bed, facing the door-way, with his back to me. My mom went back to her room down the hall. Jason suddenly got up off the bed and walked around to the stereo and turned it all the way up. This wasn't a weekend while my mom was in Vegas; this was us while the baby was sleeping and my mom was down the hall. I told him to turn that shit down, and he gave me a cold stare 'cause he was mad. We started to get into it, talking shit: "Turn that shit down." "I'm here to see my son." "I don't care, you can go home." Just yelling at each other back and forth. Quickly my mom came in the room and told him to get out. He went down the stairs first, mumbling under his breath while my mom followed him out the house, cussing him out. "YOU GOT SOMETHING TO SAY?" She slammed the door on him as soon as he walked out. I had never seen nobody talk to him like that, so I got a little kick out of him getting cussed out, because he wouldn't let nobody—kid, adult, parent, anybody—talk to him like that. So to see him get cussed out and have nothing to say was new to me.

Even with Jason and my mom having no love for each other, we didn't stay broken up long. About a month later Jason came to me with a real, genuine apology. He came over on a weekend my mom was out of town so he could apologize. For the first time he told me he was wrong, apologizing for not being present and telling me he was sorry for being in the streets and that he would be better. I wasn't about to immediately get back together off some nice words; I had to see some action in it. He asked if he could stay the night like we used to, but I quickly told him no. When he accepted it immediately and kept showing up and being the nicer person he promised to be, I saw he was genuine. He even tried to make my mom's life easier, but it would take more than a month and a wholehearted apology to win her over.

My mom had no love for the little asshole who fucked up her daughter's life. Jason's absence made everything more palatable for my mom. He was a distraction, for me and for her. In my mom's eyes, the baby was just a bump in the road that might make everything tougher, but I was still on track with honor roll and my dreams of Spelman. Jason's absence meant that I could carry on. I still wanted Jason around. I was in love, but I knew my mom was crazy. Marriage was the natural progression. I was still playing double Dutch, but now I was trying to live out the rhymes. *First comes love, then comes marriage.* We already had the baby in the baby carriage. I didn't understand why my mom didn't understand. When I asked her to sign off on me and Jason getting married, she said no.

Marriage meant I would be able to see him in jail and we would be together forever, no matter what. We only talked over the phone, and because my mom didn't support any of it, I paid for all the collect calls from jail on our phone bill.

By the summer of 1997, Jason had been in jail for almost a year. I graduated high school a year early, from a school that would let me complete high school and bring my baby to school. Tre was eighteen months old and perfect—quiet, independent, and very compassionate. He had already started walking around on his own. We moved into my granny's house after graduation so I could start community college. Jason and I still talked over the phone, and I was still paying for all the collect calls. I had just turned seventeen, and was only one year away from getting to marry Jason.

A couple months after I graduated, Jason's trial finally finished. Sentencing was scheduled, but the only updates I got were from Jason's calls.

One night Granny handed me the cordless phone in her kitchen.

"How you doin'? How's Tre?" Jason asked in a calm, steady voice.

"What happened?" I asked anxiously. "What they give you?"

"Twenty-two."

"Twenty-two what?"

"Twenty-two years," he said, still calm.

I left my body and sank to the kitchen floor, where Tre was playing with his toys. He put his hand on my shoulder, his face on my face. I kept crying.

"Stop crying," Jason said.

I couldn't stop. He couldn't start.

"Fuck!" He hung up.

I stayed on the kitchen floor with the cordless in my hand. All I could hear was the dial tone.

● ● ●

My first love was someone I'd never met: Tupac Amaru Shakur. I never knew what love felt like; my body never gave me any physical sensations on how love should feel. If anything, I felt like my heart always betrayed me when it came to love of any kind, especially with boys or men. I was used to being let down by men, especially the men in my life at that time. Tupac was the first man I felt could do no wrong. I knew I loved him because of the way my heart smiled anytime I heard him talk or give an interview about the state of the world, specifically kicking knowledge about what was going on in LA and the intentional demise of Black folks by the government, crack, or prison. How he talked with his whole chest and spoke truth to power always. Other than my cousin Kawai, Tupac made me feel like I wasn't alone in this world.

Tupac was everything I wanted to be. He was able to step into every space and be unapologetically himself. Intellectual and hood. Poet and survivor. Relentless. If you fuck with us, we will fucking destroy you. Tupac represented a West Coast dynasty; he brought so much pride to LA, and the streets loved him. I longed for that. I wanted to make a difference for my community, and I wanted to put on for my city. The truth is, both Tupac and I were looking for love in all the wrong places, and we were loyal at times to a fault. Tupac was shot in Vegas on September 7, 1996, after the Mike Tyson fight. My mom and stepdad were at the fight; they won a bunch of money betting on the fight and at blackjack afterward, so they decided to go back out to Vegas the next weekend. That next weekend I was at home, alone, waiting on Jason, watching TV, making Hamburger Helper, hoping for a good night with Jason while Tre slept and my parents were out of town. After Jason didn't show up, I ate alone, and I lay down in bed with the TV on so I could go to sleep. I found out watching the news that while I was busy making Hamburger Helper, Tupac had died in the ICU. I found out the next morning that while I was making Hamburger Helper and Tupac had died in the ICU, Jason was getting arrested.

When Tupac was murdered, it wasn't just the death of a celebrity. A little piece of me died with him; he was forever gone. I couldn't ever meet him or, hell, even visit him behind the walls. Eight months after Tupac was murdered, I graduated high school with a toddler, and Jason went to prison. I never got to visit Tupac behind the walls, but Jason's incarceration was the start of my long and intimate relationship with prisons.

LEARNING TO SWIM

Before Tre, before Jason, before Tupac, before we moved to Rosemead, before third grade, before my dad went to jail, he would come visit. With my dad there was no regular visitation schedule; he came through when he came through. On the weekends I would be at my granny's house on Courtney Street, in Watts, and every now and then he would drop by—but only if he was on the way to somewhere else, like to visit his mom or one of his homeboys. One day, the summer of 1987, I was seven, playing Chinese jump rope on the porch with Kawai. We would tie the stretchy rope that was like a giant rubber band around one of the pillars on the porch and then around one of our ankles. We jumped around, on, and through the ropes, trying more and more tricks and raising the ropes farther up our legs to see if we could jump around it. My cousins Kawai and Antwoine were my crew. We either lived together or spent time together after school on Courtney Street. Kawai stayed with us for as long as I could remember, except for the one year she lived in Orange County with my aunt. Antwoine lived with my granny in Watts, but since we spent all our time there after school and on weekends, we saw each other often. All our mail might have gone to different addresses, but we *lived* on Courtney Street.

Antwoine is six years older than me. He's the son of my granny's oldest son, who died when Antwoine was three. My granny took Antwoine in when he was in third grade, after his mom got addicted to crack. His skin is shiny and smooth, the color of an Angelino plum, the kind we devoured during the summers at our granny's house, always with a fresh bald fade with the cleanest eyebrow slits. Antwoine is street-smart, quick-tempered, and don't take no shit from anybody. Because of this, my granny sent him to stay with us after he got suspended from school for fighting. We're all close, but me and Kawai, we're tight.

Me and Kawai are twins born a year apart. People called us by one name, KeKeandKawai. We shared a crib. Plus we dressed alike, talked alike, walked alike, had the same braids, same beads. We played hide-and-seek with our neighborhood friends on Courtney Street. I loved playing cams—it's like hood pool, played in a square board about the size of a car hood that you set on top of trash cans to lie flat. The inside of the board has green felt like a pool table, but you shoot wooden checkers around the board. I didn't know the rules; I just loved to play. Summers on Courtney Street meant eating free lunches they gave out at Will Rogers Park—a thick-cut baloney-and-government-cheese sandwich on that good soft bread, with chips and a little juice. (I wiped all the mayonnaise off because I wasn't messing with no mayonnaise.) Summers meant playing house, spending all the spare change I collected from my mom and Granny at the candy house, or sitting on the front porch with Kawai, eating frozen cherry Kool-Aid ICEEs out of Styro-foam cups until our tongues were completely red.

While me and Kawai played Chinese jump rope, I heard a boom-ing bass coming down the block. I could feel the vibrations of my dad's music banging out of his speakers—every note was clean and loud because he had the best system with the best amps with the perfect settings. He always listened to rap music: Ice-T (when he was a playboy hustler, before *Law & Order*), Big Daddy Kane, Rakim, and Kool Moe Dee. "Cold-ass music," as my daddy would say.

He pulled up in front of the driveway in his El Camino, making sure everybody on the street could see it. Oh, I loved that car. He told me I could have it when I got to sixteen. In the eighties the El Camino was a cornerstone of West Coast culture. As I look back now, it might just look like a compact pickup truck, but the ElCo was everything in LA at the time. No matter what part of LA you were in, an ElCo meant money and status. You might have done street races on Florence, like my uncle Robert in his Cadillac, or just driven it around to look good, like my dad. My daddy's ElCo was all white with silver specs all over. The interior was crushed blue velvet. I loved to run my fingers over the seats, feeling each rip-ple. The way it bunched up reminded me of the ocean we saw from Venice Beach when me and Kawai played in the sand. It always felt sunny in the passenger seat. My favorite detail was the passen-ger side window: in the little triangle at the back that doesn't roll down, "KeKe" was airbrushed in stencil next to my sisters' names.

Dad left the car running with the music on so he could step out and do his pigeon-toed peacock strut. He was a hood legend, had to let everybody know he was around. He made his grand entrance in his ElCo and stepped out to do his signature dance—a two-step shuffle in place, quickly stepping, sliding, tapping his feet to his own rhythm, like he was standing behind the mic with The O'Jays or The Temptations, but with a little soft shoe next to his car. He was a clean-ass nigga. He stayed dressing fresh with super-creased-up 501s that could stand up on their own. Gator boots, some exotic-type shit, or some Stacy Adams were always on his feet; fresh-pressed button-up shirts, new shit only; always a fresh cut, bald fade. His signature Gazelle glasses. His skin dark and rich, what older folks would call blue-black. In the era of Lionel Richie, Prince, El DeBarge and Al B. Sure!—when light skin was in the spotlight—he was still confident and poppin' with an un-matched, infectious charisma. There was always a giant roll of cash rubber-banded together in his pockets. He checked all the boxes for being a hustler. Nobody had to ask what he did; everybody already knew. All the homies in the neighborhood could see how he was living, especially my momma.

I jumped off the porch and ran to my dad's car, yelling, "Granny, my daddy here!"

Granny opened the screen door to peek out just enough to make sure I was telling the truth.

My dad stood relaxed in front of his El Camino and called out, "Hey, Ms. Erma!"

"Hey, Micheal," Granny politely called back from behind the screen door. She gave a quick wave before heading back to her E&J and Marvin Gaye records.

With the courtesy check-in out the way, I called out, "Granny, I'm gonna be right back; I'm gonna take a ride with my dad." No more conversation necessary. Me, Kawai, my dad, and my granny all knew the routine. This was the time he and I got to spend to-gether, just us.

Granny was already back in the house with her music on. I was already in my dad's El Camino, and we were off. Windows down, music blasting while he drove.

He looked around, watching people watching him, searching for haters and jackers. His head was on a swivel, moving in rhythm to the music. Look straight out the windshield, check the rearview, check out my window, check out his window, back to the windshield. He was like a clock with missing numbers. Noon. One. Three. Nine. Noon. He was focused on the drive; he ain't worried about me.

My mom raised me right, so I was waiting on him to speak before I started talking. I chewed my lip and looked out the window, trying to figure out where we were going or waiting for him to tell me.

We passed by the street for my other granny's house, so we weren't going to his mom's.

I watched out the window as we passed our church, Citizens of Zion, in Compton. It was Saturday, so we weren't going to church. We didn't know anybody in Compton; that could only mean we were going to the Compton Swap Meet.

The Compton Swap Meet was the shit! Most people shopped at the mall, but in the hood, the Compton Swap Meet was the spot. It was *the* place to get the new Filas, Nike Cortezes, cassettes, dolphin earrings, Jesus pieces, Nike and MCM sweat suits, and basically anything fly. Everybody went to the swap meet—didn't matter if you were somebody, if you had dope-boy money or saved up or stole to get cash, you were there. If you wanted to look top-of-the-line, you shopped at the Compton Swap Meet or got your shit tailor-made. We weren't shopping at the mall; that shit was for white people, and the clothes there were trash. And, most importantly, there ain't no malls close to the hood. Going to the mall meant somebody had to drive at least thirty minutes to even get to the nearest one. Shopping at the Compton Swap Meet meant something. When you got *dressed* dressed, you were somebody for the day—even if it was an illusion. While you were rocking whatever you got from there, you weren't just a free-breakfast-and-lunch kid, and it didn't matter if your mom was a basehead or your pops was locked up—for that day, you was West Coast fly and not to be fucked with, at least for that moment.

Walking into the Compton Swap Meet was like entering a huge warehouse filled with probably over a hundred vendors in little booths. Each store separated by blue or green tarp or black iron bars. Walking through a maze of hood fashion, so many shops strung together, you could easily get lost, especially as a seven-year-old. It was hard not to spend the whole day in there, looking at each booth, taking it all in, not to miss anything. We got to my dad's favorite jewelry spot. I was lost in the shine of the display cases. Two-finger rings. Three-finger rings. Four-finger rings. Rings with old English initials. Diamond-cluster rings. All the grown women, when they were dressed, they got rings. Being grown meant you stacked your rings. My mom stacked her diamond clusters on her ring and index fingers, at least three per hand. Combined with nails, rings made your whole hand pop. For Black girls in LA, especially where I'm from, getting gold was a rite of passage. I had gold bracelets with my name on them; I already wore small gold earrings shaped like two dolphins, with the two tails at the clasp, starting at your ear and curling down to kiss at the bottom to form a hoop. But rings were grown-women shit. I couldn't wait to get some of my own.

"Keeonnaaa." My dad called me over. He was the only one who didn't call me KeKe, but he put his own extra pronunciation on my name, stretching out the last syllable. He'd been talking to the owner by one of the other display cases. He was leaned over, calmly pointing to the velvet cloth laid out in front of him. On the cloth was a gold rope chain with a gold heart pendant and "Keeonna" engraved across it. He was leaning, cool, pointing, like it was no big deal. For me the necklace was everything. Fourteen-karat gold. Anything fake and I would get clowned at school. It was blinding-to-the-eyes shiny, like the collection plates at Sunday morning service. This wasn't my first necklace, but it was the first one he got me. Straight from his hands to my neck. No middleman, no doubts in the back of my mind that somebody else bought it for him, no lies about how he got it for me when it was for somebody else. An unbroken chain, no kinks or questions about how I got it or who it came from. I could wear it forever.

Without speaking, he picked it up and fastened it around my neck. The chain was cold and heavy. Gold was valued by weight, and my chain weighed me down to let me know how valuable I was to him. That kind of weight was security, a constant reminder of my worth.

I looked at myself in the little round mirror on top of the case, and I was hypnotized. All I saw was the necklace, shining back at me. Things were going to be different; he was gonna spend more time with me. As long as the necklace was around my neck, my dad was with me. As I watched the necklace gleam in the mirror, shining from the fluorescent light of the swap meet, I daydreamed about all the time we were going to spend together. Just us hanging out, quality time. Before it was only quick runs to Tam's for a burger, or a few minutes with my dad at his mom's house. I could see the future in my necklace; he was going to make time. He was going to take me and Kawai to the Alondra 6 for a movie, drive us around the hood to show off, or take us to Skate Depot on a Saturday night. Skate Depot was *the* thing to do. A place where you and your friends could hang, outside of your block. But it was a twenty-minute car ride, so it wasn't a kickin' spot for everybody, 'cause everybody didn't have a car or someone to drop them off and pick them up. Movies, skating, and hanging out, all because of my necklace.

I spun around and wrapped my arms around his waist. "Thank you!"

He quietly rubbed my back, then we walked back to the car side by side. I was bouncing in my shoes, almost skipping. I hurried into the car, throwing myself into the seat and sitting up. I was ready, anticipating some more greatness. The El Camino started, music blasted out the speakers, and we were off. I chewed on my cheek, looking out the back window for landmarks. Something to say where we were going next. Once we hit Wilmington Avenue and kept going, I bit my lip hard. This was the way home. I didn't know where my dad lived, but I knew if we were going this way past Wilmington, the only place left to go was my granny's house.

He pulled up in front of the driveway, right where he had picked me up. This time he didn't have to step out.

"Aight. Well. Love you," he said, giving me a side hug. He unlocked the door and waited for me to get out.

It wasn't a day at the movies, or the skating ring, or the other million things I saw in my head at the swap meet, but at least I was back on Courtney Street and there was still daylight. I ran in the house to let Granny know I was home, and headed to the park to catch up with Kawai and the rest of the kids.

● ● ●

My mom goes by Black Gold, B, Busy B, or Bridgett. Each name has a different meaning, a different story, and signals how long she knows or how close she is to the person. My mom is short, has skin the color of cacao, with red undertones, bright, unwrinkled, smooth, and unblemished—that's how she got her name Black Gold, because she shines. Her hair always feathers perfectly, without a strand out of place. Quick-tempered, don't take no shit, a hard worker, and probably the sweetest person you will ever meet, unless you cross her. When I was growing up, my mom poured all of herself into me, like she was trying to build a better version of herself and live life over again. People still call me Lil' Bridgett.

My mom was Granny's eldest girl, born in Texas, grew up in South Central Los Angeles. Mom graduated high school and got away from the Franklin Squares in Watts. She met my dad in high school before he dropped out. She went to San Diego State University with plans of being a doctor. My dad would drive down to San Diego to visit my mom. She got pregnant with me during her freshman year and dropped out to move back home to Watts and live with my granny. After I was born, my mom went to nursing school to become a licensed vocational nurse (LVN). Once she graduated, she found out my dad had another kid on the way, back where he was from in Louisiana, so my parents broke up for good when I was two years old. She worked fifty-hour weeks at a convalescent home in Lynwood: dressing wounds, helping grown people into bed/out of bed/turning over in bed, changing bedpans, cleaning tracheostomy tubes. She started her shift in the evening. When she got home in the morning, she went right to bed. My mom loves being a nurse, and always takes pride in what she does. She was most proud of the fact that we didn't need my dad "for a motherfuckin' thing."

Part of that meant that I always looked good, dressing flyer than most adults, on the cutting edge of trends and fashion. At the time Kawai was living with us too, and my mom kept the three of us looking like a fashion house. We didn't just go back-to-school shopping; we did seasonal shopping, a hood Hilary Banks before she even existed. LA Gear, Fila sweat suits, K-Swiss, silk shirts, overalls, biker shorts, hot fashions, all the shit. We got our hair pressed, braided, beads, basket weaves, every week. My mom had me in the shop more than grown women. My favorite outfit was this turquoise leather skirt with a turquoise sweater covered in white and pink hearts. Kawai had lavender leather pants with a matching lavender sweater with white and pink hearts. We wore these on our dress-free days, when we didn't have to wear uniforms, looking more like models than kids. My mom had me and Kawai in basket weaves, hair that was too grown and expensive for some kids, but my mom let us do it anyway. When you look good, people don't ask questions about what's going on inside.

My mom dressed our house the same way she dressed us. We looked good, and the house had to stay cleaner than clean. Every Saturday meant cleaning the whole house, top to bottom. My mom's living room was like a shrine to cleanliness. We had to dust our gigantic box TV, a huge wooden unit that came up to my chest. On either side of the TV my mom had two gold cases, tall with octagon embellishments at the top, lined with glass shelves for pictures. Kawai was taller than me, so she had to dust the top while I dusted the pictures sitting on the glass shelves, and we both Windexed the whole thing. The couch was plush, black and mauve, looking like a showroom floor every day. Nobody was allowed to sit on it or mess it up. She always rolled her eyes at my granny for keeping plastic on her couch 'cause it looked tacky. My mom's solution was to just keep everyone off the couch all the time. Then came vacuuming the floor. My mom had to see the lines in the carpet to know it was done right. Better not mess them up walking through. When we watched TV, we sat on the floor, close to the TV, to make sure to not mess up the couch or the vacuum lines.

A couple years after I got my necklace, Kawai and I were cleaning the house like we did every Saturday, and my mom was getting ready to go out and run errands like she did every Saturday. She was dressed, of course, with her hair in a feather and a pressed, clean summer dress, just to run to the bank and go to the money order places to pay bills, get her car washed, and get that baby powder smell in the car. When she got back, the cleaning had to be done so we could all go to Granny's.

My mom was getting ready to walk out the door, hand on the knob, and called over to me. "Kee. Um. I know you ain't talked to your dad in a bit, but he's in jail now, for something he did when he was younger. He wrote you a letter; you can read it and write him back later." She handed me the letter and walked out the door. Just matter-of-fact. She didn't tip me off with anything in her voice, no worry, no long talks, no explanation. This wasn't no after-school special. Casual. It's not like he lived with us. He never came around that much either. If she hadn't said anything, I would've just assumed he was somewhere else in the city.

I went right back to cleaning. I understood what he did for a living. I was ten years old and could put two and two together. The only people who dressed flashy, carried rolls of money, and drove through the hood like he did were drug dealers. Sometimes dealers went to jail. My dad wasn't the first person I heard of going to jail, and my dad was so sometimey that it was just like hearing about my friend's cousin or uncle or a neighbor down the street getting arrested. I felt bad for them; it was unfortunate. But that was the game. Life went on. The biggest shock was that he was in Louisiana. I knew that was where him and his family were from, but I didn't understand why he got sent to some Louisiana jail. The weirdest part was the letter. He'd never gone out of his way to talk to me, just showing up every now and then when he felt like it, to say hi. I didn't open the letter till a couple days later.

But the letters kept coming.

They always came in a little manila envelope, a faded golden yellow like a banana Now and Later. The first letter was a shock because I had never seen my dad's handwriting before. Neat, well-spaced, clean print—like a sixth grader who takes pride in their work. I never got a birthday card, a little note, anything with his signature on it until the letters arrived. These were directly to me, not through my mom or anybody else, so I got to open them without having to ask anybody's permission.

Each letter was always one page of yellow paper, in dark pencil from pressing hard.

"Dear Keeonna," he would always start.

"How you doing?" or "How's school?" or "How are your friends?" or "What you been up to?"

Then he would write about whatever he'd been doing, trying to stretch the letter over a short paragraph. Maybe the new book he was reading, or whatever weather they had in Louisiana. Little things from his days in jail. Once he was done telling me about himself, it always ended the same.

I love you and I miss you. I can't wait to see you.

Dad

Our letters stayed simple and straightforward.

"Dear Dad, I'm doing fine." Or "School is good, I'm learning about . . ." Or "Kawai is good too." Then on to the big, exciting events from third grade, whatever me and Kawai did that week, hi from my mom, or Aunie, or Granny.

"Love, Keeonna."

I had just learned how to write letters at school, so I knew the template. My dad was my first pen pal. Letters came once, sometimes twice, a week. Every time it was the same page of "Dear Keeonna" and his updates. I replied every week with "Dear Dad" and my third-grade life. Each week I put the latest letter into my collection in a drawer until my mom bought me a little Caboodles tote, then I stored them all in the closet.

My dad was locked up in Louisiana, but this was the closest we had ever been. He couldn't take me to the movies or Skate Depot, but he could write me a letter about his day. We never got to talk on a regular basis when he was home. He was a character in a story to me. I heard more about him than I heard from him. I didn't know his favorite food, favorite color, just the day he was born. Not even the year. I knew he was older than my mom. I didn't know his dad; I'd seen his mom on holidays because my mom would take me there every Thanksgiving or Christmas. His mom lived down the street from my granny, but I only visited on holidays because my mom took me, not because his mother was sending for me or inviting me. Holidays at my dad's mom's house was a time when we got to see my dad and his mom and some of his side of the family.

But what I did know about my dad was he was a hood *star*. People would tell stories about him with a gleam and smile in their eye; he was the man. Everybody knew how he got money; everybody knew how he dressed, how many women he had. Stuff he did in the streets. He had it all. He was a shoe man. He always had the new alligator shoes, first one in the neighborhood to have something. He shopped out of state to make sure nobody in the state had what he got on. Clothes were tailor-made so he would stand out, not blend in with the rest of the broke boys. He was the type of nigga who had a car for every outfit. Now, with each letter, I felt like we were getting closer, learning more about each other. This wasn't a one-time gesture. The letters kept coming and let me know that I mattered to him.

I'd been alone for a couple months since Kawai moved out to live with her mom. It was a big transition; Kawai and I had lived together for as long as I could remember. But now that she was out in Orange County, we couldn't be on the phone too much since it was a long-distance call. We only got to meet up on Courtney Street if we were lucky enough to get dropped off on the same weekend. With my dad I had someone to talk to again. He became my new confidant, someone I could tell everything about my life. This was our new beginning. He was there when I needed some-body the most. His letters said he was interested in my life, and showed me a side I hadn't ever seen before. Writing letters back and forth, I got to know him as much as he got to know me, every week, for a whole year.

Then the letters stopped.

• • •

One night, about a month after the last letter from my dad, I woke up to get water and heard my mom crying. It was weird to hear her crying, but even weirder to hear her home at night. She was usually at work by now. Approaching her room, I wondered if it was her. I started searching around, thinking if I needed something to defend myself. I didn't want her to catch me out of bed, but curiosity got the better of me. The doorway to her room had a mini hallway, so you couldn't tell someone was near till you were all the way in the room.

I peeked in and saw someone in the room with her, so I held back. I didn't want to get caught. I peeked in further, and there she was, sitting next to my dad. It was dark outside, and the house was asleep. No TVs, no people noise outside, just the middle of the night, with streetlight coming in my mom's windows in our second-floor apartment. My mom never let men come to the house, but I recognized his silhouette. My dad is Black as midnight; nobody else I know is that dark. I could only see him from the waist up in a wifebeater.

My mom was hunched over in her little black housecoat covered in colorful flowers, softly sobbing into her hands. Even though I couldn't see the details of them, I heard my dad's voice telling her it was gonna be okay while he rubbed her back. I hadn't seen my dad in person since he bought me my necklace. He never said he was coming home in his letters, and my mom never said he was back. Anytime I saw my mom close with a man, I got a pit in my stomach and my mouth got all watery, like I wanted to throw up. I wasn't about to drink anything feeling like this, so I decided to stay out of grown-folk business and quietly slipped back to bed. When I woke up my dad wasn't there. Later that day my mom told me her car had gotten stolen during the night, and she was stuck at home.

Watching my parents together in the dark was how my mother first introduced me to silence. She had never told me to shut up, to be quiet, or to not ask questions. I learned from the way her lips curled on the left side, the fact that she didn't say anything to me or anyone else about that night or the times my father didn't show up to spend time with me. I learned from her face to not ask her any question, especially about my father.

I was taught to never question adults. Like my granny always said, "Respect your mother and father so that your days on this earth will be long." She taught me to swallow my sadness. What I knew for certain was to not question, even when your stomach is in knots. I learned to eat my tongue, to chew the inside of my cheeks and lips until they were bloody and raw. I would feast on my own flesh until it hurt to talk and eat. Ingesting bits of my own tissue made me feel in charge of my body. It made it impossible to speak ill of my father.

The hard truth about my father is that I believe he was never interested in having a relationship with me. My father got what he came for and left.

● ● ●

A few months after my dad got out of jail and disappeared to the streets again, it was my favorite time of the year: summertime. Summer in Watts as a kid was the best: we stayed at the park all day, ate free lunch, and went swimming. Will Rogers Park was around the corner from my granny's house, so my cousins and I went there every day. It was 1990, and I was ten years old, and that summer was different because my mom had signed me and Kawai up for swimming lessons. Kawai already kinda knew how to swim, but I didn't. I was excited. I had my Black-girl swim kit ready. A cute burgundy spaghetti-strap one-piece bathing suit. One of my granny's good towels. Fresh French braids with clear beads on the ends. I looked *cah-yute*.

I got up, ate breakfast, brushed my teeth, washed my face, and put on my bathing suit. Kawai and I skipped all the way to the pool—we couldn't run, but walking was too slow, so we skipped to push the limits. Our beads click-clacked in unison as our hair swung around. The smell of chlorine started down the street, but as we got closer, we heard people talking, splashing, shouting, having fun at the park on a hot summer day. The ice-cream trucks were lined up outside the gates, selling chili-cheese Fritos, chili-cheese nachos, strawberry-shortcake popsicles, and every kind of ice cream. Snacks were a rarity on school days, but weekends in the summertime meant that everybody could get snacks at the park, just to keep kids out the house a little longer. It smelled like summertime.

As we walked up, I could see the outlines of people through the fence. It was a sea of brown buoys, little heads bobbing in the water. Kawai and I signed in and put our little bag with our clothes and flip-flops in the locker. Kawai pinned the key to her swimsuit. We walked out to the pool. The pool itself was a huge rectangle with a low and high diving board, with no dividers or real lifeguards. The smell of chlorine was so strong, it would sting your eyes the second you walked in. It was swim at your own risk, but everyone wanted to be there. Especially in the summertime: it was nice and hot out, plus we got free lunch, so you could stay there all day while your parents were at work. It felt like a safe place, filled with kids from the block, everyone you went to school with. Everybody knew one another; kids could be at the park without worry.

I was so happy to learn how to swim! Now I could play Marco Polo with Kawai and go beyond three feet deep. Our swim instructor was a young average dude from Watts. Probably around twenty years old, caramel complexion with a Jheri curl, and dark brown swim trunks. First thing to do was to grab ahold of the side of the pool and kick our legs. It was not as easy as I thought. As soon as I kicked my legs out, they sunk. After ten minutes of kicking (and sinking), we got out of the pool and lined up in a single-file line.

The instructor stood in the pool and told us to jump. He held his arms out, ready to catch us. I was skeptical because I'm scared of the water. I'd never been past three feet deep; I didn't let the water get near my shoulders. But the instructor swore he'd catch me. He wanted us to learn to be unafraid of the water. I was near the back, so I heard kid after kid jump in safely. I closed my eyes and thought it should be easy enough, but my stomach was in knots. I told myself, *It'll be okay. You can do this, Keeonna. He's got you.*

I jumped.

The water rushed over my head. I couldn't breathe. I panicked and started flopping around. I struggled in the water, tried reaching for something, anything. Finally, the instructor pulled me up and put me at the edge of the pool.

"You said you were gonna catch me!" I yelled.

"I wanted you to experience putting your head underwater." He shrugged.

Angry, I stomped back to the towel claim. I didn't tell Kawai or anybody I was leaving. The instructor was a liar. I left the mesh bag full of our stuff behind the counter; Kawai had the key. I wasn't waiting for nothing. I wrapped myself in my towel and decided I was going home, beads clicking and clacking as I stomped out of Will Rogers Park. My feet burned against the hot concrete, but I wasn't stopping. Granny's house was only a block away.

At Granny's door I paused. I needed to fix my face before I went inside. I was still mad and didn't need any questions. I opened the door slowly and made a beeline for the bathroom. I locked the door behind me before Granny noticed. My little one-piece clung to my skin the way it was supposed to, but I wanted it off. It was like peeling off a layer of dead skin, slow and uncomfortable. I finally got it off and showered, rinsing off the chlorine, and the pool, and the park—all of it.

I didn't trust swim instructors or the water. How could I trust anything that was see-through; how could I trust it could hold me? I was *done*. Done with men lying, saying they would catch me, and done believing something I couldn't see would keep me afloat.

● ● ●

That swim lesson became a life lesson for me. That was the day I awakened to my life and my environment. That was the day it clicked that I couldn't trust people. I would have to learn to float on my own before I started swimming. I wasn't going to jump into anything feet-first, and I wasn't about to trust someone to catch me. I wasn't going to become a swimmer; after that, I tried to become the water. I became the colorless, see-through, and odorless liquid that is the basis for living. I held up my granny, my mama, my daddy, my aunie, my cousin, and later, Jason. I'd never let their lungs fill up with water; I'd never let them suffocate. I kept them afloat. I let them lie on my back, and I carried them safely to shore. I let them ingest me until they were full. I was the giver of life and a source of nourishment. They needed me to survive; three days without me and they would die.

I didn't learn to swim until I turned thirty-eight, after Will Rogers Park became Ted Watkins Park. After I moved to Arizona and learned at Pecos Park in Ahwatukee. I lay atop the water, eyes to the sky, and I didn't sink. I knew then that I didn't need anyone to catch me, to provide nourishment, or to breathe life into me. I knew that as long as I loved and trusted myself, I would always rise to the top.

FISHING

In prison they call writing letters "going fishing." You wrap your letter on a piece of string and throw it out the cell, cast it out, and drag it to wherever it needs to be.

After Jason got arrested I started getting them again. I was sixteen years old receiving letters from LA County's Men's Central Jail. Over that year, Jason sent me letters with little sketches on the outside of the envelope: a teddy bear, "J+K," little hearts. In 1996 the only other option was a collect call. The one time I let Jason call collect, I figured I could pay my mom back. Figured it couldn't be more than seventy-five dollars; we weren't talking more than ten minutes at a time. I let him call me two or four times a week. The phone bill that month was over four hundred dollars. I got lucky that my mom didn't cuss me out because I warned her it was gonna be high and that I would get the money to pay her back from one of Jason's friends. That was a lie, but I figured out how to get the money afterward, and thankfully, she didn't trip. But I wasn't doing that again. Phone calls were for family emergencies only.

Letters were our lifeline as Jason and I figured out our relationship. We knew each other, or we thought we knew each other, before he went to jail. We were starting a family. We wanted to be a family together, so we'd figure it all out. Knowing what each other was doing, our wants and needs. Our letters carried our moods. The way we addressed them expressed how we felt. They carried energy. Cursive for kindness, taking the time to make it fancy and flowery. Print for anger, letters blocked out. Prison stopped us from talking over the phone because it was too expensive, and visiting was out of the question because I was a minor. I couldn't get a ride or permission to go visit him in jail. So we wrote.

1996
Dear KeeKee Espinoza,
    I'm so glad I got your letter. . . . I'm glad to hear you and Tre are doing well. You guys are always with me. . . . I can't wait for us to get married, and grow old together. . . .

> Your Husband,
> Jason Espinoza

- -

1996
Dear Jason,
    I miss you so much. . . . I can't wait for you to come home and we can get married. . . .

> Love,
> KeKe

We weren't married, but our early letters were our honeymoon period. The wait between letters was nerve-wracking. You saved up what to say between letters and you didn't want to forget. If you had good news, once you sent it off, you waited for a reaction to share the joy. Arguments are also a wait. If they said something slick in a letter and you had to fire back, you had to wait for their response, apology, or retort. Letters gave you distance, when you could really sit with your feelings. Letters gave me a chance to really think about what I wanted to say. Good or bad, letters were always a wait.

1997

Dear Kee Kee Espinoza,

I hope this letter finds you and our son in the best of health. Before I continue, I wanna apologize for the phone cutting off mid-conversation yesterday. Moving forward I won't ask you to make any three-way calls for me when I do call.

So how are you doing? How's Tre? I'm sorry I missed your graduation, but I'm very proud of you. I got the pictures of Tre. He's getting really big. It's crazy how time flies.

I just got my appeal papers in the mail. It means it was filed with the court of appeals. I'm so happy. All we need to do is keep praying about it so I can come home. So if you can, see if you can get in contact with the lawyer. If you can get ahold of him, maybe you can write something or come up to the court to talk on my behalf.

Babe, you really made me feel good inside when you said that you would rather be with me sometimes then not in my life at all. You know I need Kee Kee all the time. But this is just something that happened, and I need to grow from it. I love you more every day. Even though I can't call you and see you and Tre, I miss y'all and love y'all every second.

I picked up this book. It's about this sista named Assata Shakur. You should read it. It's deep. I was thinking all night about the book. It's such a mean world. I'm always worried about you and Tre. I would hate for some shit like what happened to her to happen to me.

I'm gonna go 'head and close this letter because they about to pick up mail. I love you and Tre with all my heart and soul. Enclosed is a visitation form and a form for stuff I can have in a package. 'Cause I need some stuff. Give Tre a kiss for me.

Your Husband,

Jason Espinoza

1997

Dear Jason,

I was glad to get your letter. I'm glad the appeal was filed. I'm gonna call the attorney this week, so I can talk to him to see what I need to do to help you come home.

Guess who showed up at my graduation? Micheal Harris. Funny, huh? I was happy to graduate, but it sucked because you weren't there with me. And Kawai wasn't there because our graduations were the same day. So I felt alone. But the good thing is, me and my mom and Bert went to Red Lobster. That was bomb. I know you jealous, fatty, haha.

I think I'm gonna go to junior college, probably Southwest. I'm gonna ask Granny if I can stay with her, so she can watch Tre while I go to school.

The book that you were talking about sounds cool. When

I get a chance and everyone gone to work and I won't get kicked off the internet, I'm gonna see if I can order the book.

Tre is getting really big. He's driving me crazy; he's all over the place. I have enough money in my savings now to get a car, so I'm gonna see if I can get a car. But I need to hurry up and try to get my license. When my next check comes, I'll order your package, and I'll call your sister and see if somebody could go in with me.

I hope to talk to you soon.

I love you.

Love,

KeKe

We knew how to stay afloat outside, and we knew we were going to figure out our stuff outside. But once prison got involved, everything was different. We still thought the appeal was going to work, he would get to come home, and we would get married on the outside. I had only heard of people getting twenty years if they killed somebody; this had to be a mistake. This was crazy. I later found out they offered him a deal, and he didn't take it because fourteen years sounded too long. We were naïve about the system and what prison would take from us.

After his conviction, Jason was moved from the downtown LA jail to a prison in Susanville, California—far as fuck north, basically in Oregon, but still in California. It was too far to drive to regularly. Fourteen hours didn't leave enough time to actually visit after I finished work. If I flew out, the only option was to go to Reno, rent a car, and then do a two-hour drive from there. Phone calls were still expensive. Then I had to figure out somebody to watch Tre. I wasn't sure about what it was like visiting and wanted to figure things out after a few times before I started bringing Tre with me. I was seventeen with an eighteen-month-old baby. My mom was always busy working, my aunt was out living her own life, and I didn't want to hear a lecture from my granny or Granny Matthews—I had enough judgment swirling around in my own head. This was a lot. This was the first time somebody so close to me was so far away. My dad and uncle were in another state and we were not close, so the time away didn't faze me. People I grew up with caught twenty, twenty-five years, but we weren't so close that I would be visiting them; those were Antwoine's friends, and I knew them and knew it was fucked up how long they were getting sentenced under the harsh punishments for selling crack. Jason was different. I was frustrated with the distance but frustrated with myself. I kept the pregnancy, had the baby. I wanted him to know his father and have a relationship because I knew how fucked up it was to feel like that. I knew Jason was sentenced to jail, but I felt like I was being punished. Things kept getting worse and worse and worse. My mom always used to tell me, "Keep doing that shit and see what you get." And this was what I got. I felt like God was punishing me for having sex, and I had brought this on myself. Twenty years that Jason would spend way up in Susanville, North Pole, California.

So Jason and I lived our lives in letters.

We spent so much time trying to figure everything out that his first year flew by. Jason became acclimated to prison life; I got acclimated to adulthood.

1998

Keeonna,

Before I go on with this letter and before you start reading, I would like all your attention focused on what I have to say.

It's real important that you listen. So if you're busy at the moment, stop reading, and continue when I have your full attention.

First, I want to apologize for my immature attitudes toward you. But I had my reasons. When I was in county jail, I asked if you would be able to deal with me in prison. And you said yes, you would. I didn't believe you would. But I rolled with it and put my trust in you anyway.

The reason I'm upset with you is 'cause I feel like you been lying to me. When you said you ran into my friends and they gave you a hundred dollars for Tre, that was a lie. Either you was already with them, or you was with somebody who knows them. So you was around them, period. And you can't tell me no different.

Also, the last letter you sent me had a number on the envelope that you tried to erase. But you didn't erase it good enough. It was probably some boy's number.

So I'm gonna ask you one more time to keep it real and tell me the truth. I just believe that I have the right to know. I won't be mad at you; I just would rather know the truth.

If you're out there dating other guys, please keep them away from my son. At least do that for me. I feel like I came at you like a man, and I expect you to come at me like a woman. You are eighteen now.

> I'm out.
> JMack

PS
Please don't write "until pen meets paper" at the end of your letter. I can't stand when you write that.

1998

Dear Jason,

I hope you're well. Tre is doing good. I'm doing good. You're trippin'. Like I said, I ran into your friends. They gave me a hundred dollars, and I bought diapers for Tre. It's hurtful that you think that I would actually be low-key trying to holler at your friends. And you already knew I went to Summer Jam and I wasn't talking to nobody. But if I was, why would I have a letter with me to write someone's number on it? It doesn't even make sense.

You're really trippin'. And you don't know what you want to do because you already told me the last time I talked to you on the phone to go on with my life. So even if I was talking to somebody, that don't have nothing to do with you because I will always love you and always have love for you. I would **never** talk to your friends. That's some ho shit.

You always tell me how you think I'm a great mom, and then you want to tell me not to have Tre around niggas. So you're really telling me how you feel about me.

Love,

KeKe

1998

Keeonna,

As always I send my utmost respects to you.

Well, I'm going to make this kite as brief as possible because I don't want to waste any of your time from this point forward.

As you know, life has no guarantees. And I know this from experience. There comes a point in time when it's best for a change in one's life, like yourself. Now please understand this has nothing to do with you. I have caused you enough pain to last you a lifetime. And I don't want to do you like that no more.

Like I told you before, I'm always going to love you because you're the mother of my son. And you have done an excellent job with raising Tre. I cannot and will not take that from you.

But I decided that it would be best for me to let you go on with your life, and Imma go on with mines. And again, it's not you.

I don't want you to be upset because I'm saying all this. Because to get you angry is my last intention.

On my son's life, this will be the last letter I ever write you, Keeonna Harris! I will write your granny to see how my son is doing out there.

I wish you the best of success, happiness, love, all of that in life.

PS

May your unborn seed
Come to this world
Strong and healthy!

1998

Dear Keeonna,

Watts up. I called. You didn't answer. Nobody answered. You can't even handle that. You could have let me know.

Maybe I'm trippin'. Maybe you got a reason not to be at
home, but you shoulda let me know.

I'm out.

Jason

This was some bullshit. I was in my first year of junior college.
I went to class all day while Tre was at day care, came home, made
dinner, fed Tre, bathed, ironed his clothes for the next day, did any
homework I could till Tre fell asleep, then finished my homework
and finally opened my letters. I never opened the letters till night-
time, when I had time to myself to really read and think about
the letter. I got to sit with my feelings, by myself, for better or for
worse. This. Was. Some. Bullshit. Everything in the letter was what
he thought, what he heard, while I was out here by myself. I had
changed my whole life plan. I was supposed to be premed at Spelman; instead, here I was, by myself, living with my granny, filling
out all my financial aid for junior college on my own by myself,
trying to keep lines of communication open with him so we could
have a relationship and he could have a relationship with Tre. And
instead, the letters now were about shit he made up in his head, or
some shit he heard through the grapevine. The only good thing I
had in my life right now was Tre—Kawai was off at college, with
her new car from her mom. We were supposed to make it out together. She was at San Diego State, playing D1 basketball. Her life
was two-a-days, school, and more school, and playing basketball.
She didn't have time for a phone call. I was happy for her, I was
proud of everything she accomplished, and I was not about to in-
terrupt that for her. But we were both supposed to be gone at college. Instead, I was here, living at my granny's house.

Every day when I came in the door, the first pictures I would see were my and Kawai's graduation pictures. They were on the wall right as you walk in the door to show off our accomplishments. Kawai's picture was her in her cap-and-gown graduation robes, with a little, smaller superimposed picture of her in her favorite silk green shirt with her basketball in the corner. My picture featured a headshot of me in my cap and gown, with a little, smaller superimposed baby picture of Tre in the corner. Antwoine's picture was just a regular picture of Antwoine—he didn't need a special accomplishment to make the wall of fame. He was always enough for my granny. Kawai had her basketball, and I had my baby. Every day walking in I had to walk past the pictures, a reminder of how I was supposed to be next to Kawai in the pictures and off at college like Kawai in real life. Instead, it made me walk by my shame. The letters were my little morsels of happiness at the end of a long day, and now it was some bullshit. What the fuck was I gonna do?

I was gonna try and make it work. I put the letter in a drawer with every other letter he wrote. He spent the year making accusations about my character, low-key calling me a ho or a bad mom, accusing me of talking to his friends or having niggas around Tre. Meanwhile, I was starting out at junior college, still living with my granny. But I was still in love with Jason. I spent the night chewing my lip, staring at the ceiling, going over his words in my head. I was eighteen, and the love of my life was ripped away. I didn't yet have words for how I was feeling. And I was scared to tell Jason what was going on inside me. I don't think he knew what to say either. We talked around each other.

Sometimes I returned to the letters and read them again. It wasn't like when we argued in person or over the phone, where you could say something in the heat of the moment and it was the passion. Letters stayed the same forever. This wasn't the first, or the last, time he'd told me to go on with my life. It wasn't the first or last time he would send me letters going off on me right after he said he wished me well.

He spoke to my mom and Granny to check up on Tre. And the whole time I was still in love with someone I couldn't be with. Why have a conversation, why try to put down my feelings into words if nothing came out of it? He threatened to take his love away and told me to move on, but once I tried something new, he came back with accusations.

His appeal was over. We lost. The twenty-year sentence was still ahead. We were both still teenagers that were figuring out our own emotions, not knowing how to deal with sadness. Jason was a twenty-year-old boy who couldn't cry in public, and the only way we could talk was over the phone, in front of everybody in prison. A gang member in prison couldn't be on the phone whining and crying. Couldn't be sad, so he got mad. All the sadness turned into anger, and sometimes it was directed at me. We went through things we couldn't or didn't know how to talk to each other about. He told me to move on, then demanded to know what I'd been up to.

When you're eighteen, twenty years feels like a life sentence. The idea that he wouldn't be home till I was in my thirties was an eternity. I wanted to be with him, but I couldn't because he was up in Susanville. But I also didn't want to be alone. I got Tre and responsibilities, but no one there for just me. In my head I was looking for people to fill time and space while Jason was away. In my head we were still together; everyone else was just until he got home. So I casually dated.

In 1998 Jason and I were not on the best terms because of the circumstances—angry with the world turned into angry with me.

I still loved him, but we were not together, and he was not coming home anytime soon. My dream of a regular family life at home with me and Jason and Tre was long deferred. So Jason and I were broken up, and I was bored and lonely. Dating with a baby was already tough enough, and so I casually dated, or as casual as you can get dating with a two-year-old. I went through a couple short relationships, nothing serious, just placeholders. Mr. Right Now. I was still thinking that when Jason got home, I was gonna be with Jason. I still loved Jason. I knew that even though he was being an asshole, he was mad at the situation. Who wouldn't be? That didn't mean he could take it out on me, but I would be pissed too. I understood him, even if he didn't understand me. So I broke up with the Mr. Right Now boyfriend after two months, started seeing a new Mr. Right Now. We casually dated for a couple months, but we messed around and I got pregnant. I debated staying with him, but quickly realized I really didn't want to be with him, but I wanted to keep my baby. I broke up with Mr. Right Now Number Two, but I was scared to tell my mom about my pregnancy and even more scared to tell Jason. We were broken up, but I knew he would take this as a personal attack, like I didn't care about him. The baby was almost born by the time I told him about it over the phone. I didn't write back or talk to him until I visited in person the next year, after the baby was born.

This would be my first time visiting Jason in prison—I'd seen Jason in jail and visited my uncle in prison and my cousin Antwoine in prison a few months before. Eamon, my new baby, was less than six months old and stayed home with his father. That meant my mom, Tre—who was now a little over three years old—and I driving fourteen hours from LA to Susanville. Tre and Jason had seen each other in jail, so this could be the first time that Tre would remember actually visiting Jason in person. Now that Jason was actually settled and stationed in a prison, we got to stay for six hours in person, where Jason and Tre could actually play, and Jason could actually pick Tre up and spend quality time. We got a cheap room at a cheap motel in the town. Susanville is a prison town, a Mayberry from hell, where everything is mom-and-pop, built for truckers passing through, people who work at the prison, and people like me, just coming for a weekend visit. Each motel, restaurant, pharmacy, everything is family-owned and -run, a little old lady at the counter in an apron straight out of the 1950s. The town would be in black and white if it wasn't real life.

I was so nervous to visit. Jason and I hadn't seen each other in person in over a year, since he got sent up to High Desert State Prison in Susanville. Last time we saw each other was in the LA jails, which meant glass between us and fifteen minutes at a time. Now we would get to be in the same room and actually see each other. But I was scared and nervous. I was scared because I still loved him, but while we were broken up, I had a whole baby with someone else. I was nervous because I felt like he was going to tell me he didn't love me anymore. Young Keeonna knew she still wanted to be with this person. Even though we had broken up, even though I had a baby with someone else, was he going to smile when he saw me? Was he going to talk at all? Was he going to be mean, call me all kinds of names? Or would he just hold everything back? I was scared of what I didn't know.

High Desert State Prison is a level-four prison, so when we went to check in to our visit, I found out the prison was back on lockdown. At that point the prison had been on lockdown for basically the whole year, so nothing but glass visits. I wasn't about to drive all that way to see him behind glass again. I was ready to see him in person. But prison was prison. They didn't give a fuck if you came from all the way around the world; there were no in-person visits during lockdown. So even though we drove all that way, there was no in-person visit during lockdown, and we got thirty minutes behind glass. Just like back at the LA jail, but with double the time seeing each other behind glass.

Weirdly, visiting High Desert in Susanville was an easy process. Nobody was driving that far for visits every weekend, so there were maybe three cars in line in front of us to get in to visit. Getting on to prison grounds, checking in with guards, was seamless and easy. Nobody else was around. Once we got in and registered, that's when we found out the prison was still on lockdown, and so we took the glass visit because we were already here and it was already a fucked-up situation. They assigned us to a booth—same setup as the county jail, a glass booth with phones—and we sat and waited for them to bring him out. After about ten minutes they brought out Jason. He was suddenly skinny; he had lost his teenage baby face and turned into a young man. I had never seen him that thin. He had been a little doughboy the last time I saw him, so seeing him now as a skinny young man threw me off. He had a mean look on his face, ice-cold. No smile. No warmth. Like I was a nobody. He mean-mugged me and smiled once he saw Tre. I picked up the phone first, "Hi!" in a regular, happy tone. He was monotone. "Put Tre on the phone." I got it, he was pissed we only got the thirty minutes and I was too, but I checked him quick. "Don't be rude, you can at least speak and say hi. You're being disrespectful." He got quiet and put his head down. He was a kid again. He knew he was wrong, but he also knew he couldn't double down because my mom was there. We restarted. He said hi in a regular but still bland voice.

I held up the phone for Tre, and they talked and smiled. Tre talked his baby talk back, but I had no idea what Jason was saying because the phone was at Tre's ear. He got on the phone with my mom for a little bit, just shooting the shit and checking in. He motioned to my mom to speak to me, and she stepped to the side with Tre so we could have the illusion of privacy. She couldn't go anywhere—we were still stuck in the visiting area for the thirty minutes—so she moved out of Jason's line of sight so we could have some privacy.

When we talked, Jason asked me about Tre. "What's he like?" or "What does he like playing with?" He really didn't ask me anything about me, just "Where's your baby?" I told him Eamon had stayed home, but Jason only rolled his eyes. Everything was off and weird. No pleasantries, nothing. Finally, out of nowhere, "Let me see your shoes?" I had on some navy sweats, a black concert shirt, and I stood up to show him my brand-new Reeboks. They were the Shroud, a black-and-white shoe with a black spandex sleeve that zipped up to cover the laces from the toe to the top. I loved them because they looked new and never seen; I had all the Jordans and Huaraches. I thought nothing of it and showed off my shoe, standing to lift my right foot up to the little countertop so he could see the design. I thought he just wanted to see the shoes; after all, he was behind the times and had no info on what the new hot shoes were. About five years later, once we were back together and decided to get married, I found out that even though at the time he was mad as hell and didn't want to talk, I looked good and he just wanted me to open up my legs so he could take a look and hope to see a print or something in between. Thirty minutes was over fast. I was already annoyed; it didn't make sense to pay another night at the hotel for another thirty minutes the next day, so we went back to the hotel, packed up, and drove the fourteen hours back to LA. A few days later Jason called. They were off of lockdown, and he could use the phone again. He had fixed his attitude in the few days after the visit, enough for a quick check-in. But I was working full-time with two little kids. I wasn't able to catch phone calls easily, so we went right back to writing letters.

1999

Keeonna,

Here goes a subscription for Vibe. I already filled it out for you. I checked it for the two-year deal for $17.95. I hope that's cool with you. Tell Treveon I said I love him. Give him a kiss for me. I'm out!

C.K.

I appreciate everything you do for me.

Respectfully,

Y.G. J. Maeksta

I sent Jason the occasional short letter with artwork from Tre's preschool. Tre was about to turn four, smart and charming.

1999

Keeonna,

Hey, what's up witcha? My apologies for taking so long to respond back. I got caught up in a few things, but that's irrelevant. I'm glad to know that everything is good with your health. Thank you for letting me know that.

Oh! No disrespect to you or your man when I called. I didn't mean to intrude. I just wanted to holla at my son and make the three-way call for my homeboy. Thank you for sending me Tre's

artwork; he got skills already. I know he's sharp by the way
we talk on the phone. He answers everything I ask him. You're
doing a supreme job of raising him.

I'm 'bout to go to the day room so I'm going to end this
note. Keep ya head up, no matter how hard times get. This is
your baby daddy, signing off. I'm out!

Respectfully,
Y.G. JMack

I learned to read Jason's mood and mindset in the letters. Each
letter was a different personality. Sometimes he used the language
of the contrite, reformed man, with a passive-aggressive business
casual. He used a nice, formal cursive print, with a precision and
care in his calligraphy like he was trying to win points with the
teacher. Other times he was mad and upset, so his tone and writing
took on his aggression, and he slipped into his gangbanger self. His
calligraphy switched to gang-styled Old English, a mix of block
letters and swooping lines with harsh angles, crossing out every C
or just leaving it out altogether. He put his anger into the texture
of his writing and showed his Blood affiliation proudly. I knew he
was actually happy and being nice when he dropped all the formal fonts. When he wrote in a clean print, carefully-written-and-
spaced letters, there was no bullshit underneath, just a joke here or
there, sincere questions, and genuine concern.

Whatever Jason was going through showed up in the letters. He
was in a level-four prison with people who had life sentences, as a
young, little guy. By this point he had built himself a reputation to
stay safe and to establish himself at the prison. His letters varied
based on his mood and got more spaced out over time. I would
catch a call on the weekend here or there. He started writing to me

every day when he first got locked up; he didn't have any money on his books, but they would give him paper and stamps for free so he could write as much as he wanted. But now that we were a few years into his sentence, he was established in prison, so he started to cut himself off from me more and more. We had already split up, but we were staying in contact. He was trying to get over me, just like I was trying to get over him. I was dealing with enough shit on my own in the real world, so the letters got further apart. I kept all my relationships to myself; I got into a serious relationship, and I was still afraid to tell Jason. Even though Jason and I were not together, I still loved him and worried about what he thought about me and us. We both tried to get on with our lives, but we would still write back and forth every now and then. A letter here and there over the next couple years. He kept dropping a note and checking in on me. The letters weren't even always to me; sometimes he would write my mom or my granny just to check in on Tre.

2001

Dear Jason,

I hope that you're well by the time this letter reaches you. Tre and Eamon are good. I'm upset with you because you keep going through my mom or Granny to check on Tre. I'm Tre's mom. I think it's disrespectful that you completely dismiss me when checking on Tre. I know that we don't get along all the time, but if you want to know how he is doing, you ask me. I'm the person who's raising him and dealing with him every day. If the shoe was on the other foot, you would be super upset if I did that to you.

I would really like us to try to get along. I don't have anything against you. I don't want Tre to grow up thinking

that we don't like each other or we don't care about each
other.

Write me back as soon as you get this letter.

Love,
KeKe

- -

2001

Keeonna,

How are you? I hope everything is good on your end. So.
Here we are again. Working to get this mother-father relationship
together. At least we continue to try. Because most mothers and
fathers don't even put forth the effort. We'll get it right one day.

I understand that you want to feel appreciated, but
sometimes you can be mean toward me. Which, in a sense,
is understandable. But you have to work on you just a little.
Like, sometimes when we're talking, it turns into you yelling
at me and hanging up the phone. Which doesn't make the
situation any better. Communication is key. And I want to get
this thing right once and for all.

I will admit that a lot of what you said makes sense. And I
take it the wrong way. But after analyzing your point of view,
I can see where you're coming from.

Thank you for your time. It is appreciated, as you are. Get
back to me as soon as possible.

From,
Young J Meezzy

We mended our relationship again, not the first time and not
the last. What was different now was we were actually staying

in touch. Being cordial. Toward the end of the year, we got back together for real, and talked about getting married. It didn't work out because I was scared. This time it wasn't on him; it was on me. I lost my job on some bullshit. It was a real job with benefits, and a pension, and good pay, and possible mobility. Losing that job was like a kick in the chest. My job stopped, but the bills didn't. I had day care, rent, a car note, car insurance, gas, food, all kinds of bills to take care of. Plus two kids. And I couldn't ask my mom for help because she was already working crazy hours to pay all her own bills. I could reach out and ask her for help and money, and I knew she would say yes. But I also knew that meant she would go pick up a third shift to work to pay my bills on top of her bills. So now I had to quickly switch the whole game plan. I found a new job quick, but it was across town, and that meant I was going to have to ask for help. I turned to my granny because she was the only one in my family who was not working and had her own car. I moved in with my granny so she could drop my kids off at school and pick them up for me.

But everything with Granny was transactional; a favor from Granny meant I owed her. I gave her my Chevron credit card so I could pay her gas for taking my boys to school, then on top of that, I gave her three hundred dollars a month for rent and I bought the groceries for the house. Now I was back on Courtney Street, living with my granny, working ten a.m. to seven p.m. But leaving Watts to get to Irvine meant I was out of the house at eight a.m. to get to work on time, and I was not getting home till eight p.m. I was at work, in traffic, barely seeing my kids. Five days a week. Weekends meant I finally got time with the kids but also meant I had no time for myself because I already had my granny watching over my kids all week, so I couldn't be asking her to watch them on the weekends.

My granny had her first son at seventeen and would always tell me how her mom said, "You had 'em, you raise 'em." This was her form of birth control, making sure I wasn't going back out or able to get pregnant again if I was working all week and taking care of kids on the weekend. I got to sneak out on the weekends if I could get a good weekend with Granny Matthews, Kawai's grandma on her dad's side. Granny Matthews was the only one who didn't ask me a million questions, just always said, "As long as you pick them up before I go to church on Sunday."

On paper I'm self-reliant, taking care of myself, I-N-D-E-P-E-N-D-E-N-T, if you know what I mean. A two-hour drive each way to work meant I got nothing but time to think about my life. Almost the picture of the ideal woman. But every day came back to the same message: "Shit, bitch. This ain't it." So I resolved myself to go back to school. I saw my mom's and aunie's relationships, and to me they had that independent life, but with a man on their arms at the family functions or when we get together. I wanted the dreamy TV family on my internal list: married by twenty-five, a house by thirty. I wanted a partner who I could live with, and not live transactionally. I was tired of biting my tongue, giving something up to make sure that family helped me out. Everything with my family came with something—a comment, a favor owed, a constant reminder that they were "helping" me out, and if I wasn't giving them what they wanted, that help would disappear. The man was just that extra something that was used to signal completeness. I dreamed of a man that I could ask for help without it getting thrown in my face or owing a debt. I thought that man was Jason, but he couldn't show up. I was twenty-one, and I didn't want my mom to tell me I was crazy. I had a second son, and I didn't want his father to take me to court and try to get custody and use my marriage to Jason against me. I already felt shame about being twenty-one with two kids. Getting married to Jason would be part of a long list of disappointments and expectations that I hadn't lived up to.

So we broke up again, but surprisingly, we stayed close. Over the next few years, we supported each other in ways we hadn't before. We kept writing letters, and our relationship started fresh. The scorched-earth tactics we used to take in our relationship were gone. We'd let down a lot of barriers. Instead, we became people who could talk to each other about everything. Neither of us had someone who we could be totally vulnerable with. My work stress, my health issues, my friendships all went into our letters. He told me about his life, his stresses in the prison, what he had to go through. Now that there was no romantic relationship fucking things up, we could finally be ourselves with each other. Jason and Kawai were the only people I could totally unmask with. The thing about having kids young and having kids before all your other friends is now there are things they can't relate to. It was hard not to have anyone around to confide in; everything was reduced to visits. Kawai was off at college in the Bay, and Jason was still in Susanville. Kawai didn't have time to sit on the phone, and Jason's calls were always expensive. Once I got my granny or Granny Matthews to watch Tre on a weekend when Eamon was with his dad. I got to visit Jason in Susanville once, and Kawai in Berkeley once. Luckily, Jason got to see Tre a couple of times while I was working, when my mom and Granny took Tre up, and I was back at home in LA. Even those times when I got to stay in LA by myself, that meant dealing with work, dealing with the aftermath of my other romantic relationships—the disgruntled baby daddy of my second son, ending a two-year relationship with someone who I thought for a moment could be the new person in my life. When I got to see Kawai at college was my chance to feel normal. We stayed in her apartment that the school provided to her because she was on the basketball team. I had imagined college as a TV show: a dorm with twin beds, roommates, and shared space. Kawai had a whole-ass apartment; it was grown. Full kitchen. Hardwood floors. Not the cinder block box I saw on TV. This was right by campus, better than I had imagined. No kids, no burdens, no favors owed. This was what life was supposed to be. We went to the club, went shopping, went out to eat. This was the life I felt like I was supposed to live. Seeing the freedom in Kawai's life at college brought something out of me.

Kawai finished college and moved back to LA so we would go to clubs, have fun, and go out. I was young, but I had two kids. So I didn't have the luxury of going out, but Kawai being around pushed me out of my comfort zone to just be me and have fun. And once Kawai was home, I didn't have to deal with all the questions from the family. If Kawai said, "We're going out this weekend," and I told Granny I was going out with Kawai, there were no questions, no burdens, no lectures. Kawai was safe, the smart one who went to college. Me and Antwoine was the fuck-ups. He was in prison, and I had babies. Saying you were going out with Kawai was like getting the best chaperone, who everybody trusted. What my family didn't know was how much fun we had. I got to be myself and not be judged. We went to the club and danced all night long. Drinks until we were buzzed, and drifting across the street from the club to get taquitos with guacamole. I got to meet new people, out of the neighborhood, outside the family, in the real world. We got out of Watts and went to the Century

Club, Peanuts, The Catch, Jerry's Deli. We got to see what life was possible beyond work, my granny's house, and home. All the spots that were *the* spots in the LA nightlife for anybody who was anybody in the LA scene.

With Kawai I got out of the house, no questions asked, and got out of my comfort zone. We danced all night, made out with randoms on the dance floor that didn't mean nothing, just moving to be happy and just vibe. When Kawai came home from college, this meant we were going out twice a month. Kawai didn't work at the phone company that my aunt worked at, the job I got fired from. Kawai refused. She wanted her own life; she was working as an intern at an independent record label and doing photography on the side until it became her full-time job. Nobody in my family understood why Kawai didn't take the job at the phone company, but nobody talked shit to her face. They might have said she was crazy or silly behind her back, but never to her face. I was proud. She didn't do what the family wanted for her; she followed her own dreams and did what she wanted unapologetically. She didn't try to make excuses to her family or try to do what I did—doing what my family said I should do and doing what I wanted on the side. Going out with Kawai opened up my life. I wasn't searching for somebody anymore, either to fill time or be that person in my life; I was just enjoying myself and having friends. I had been going to junior college in Irvine, but because of my commute and kids and work, I dropped into class late sometimes, and my teachers weren't hearing any of my reasons. I finished up my semester at Victor Valley College and stopped. I focused on work, but then I got fired from Verizon. I was having too much fun, and my work attendance slipped. I had started calling off, being late. This time I got fired I actually understood. I wasn't trippin'. The day I got fired, I sat right back at my desk to finish my KFC lunch before I packed up my stuff for good. I had to start my game plan over again.

A friend from an old job told me about a new company that was hiring; it was close to my mom's house and had better pay and benefits than Verizon. I moved out of the house with my granny and moved in with my mom in Glendora, not far from my new job. I got out from the daily surveillance and guilt of Granny to my mom. My mom had her own rules, but she was working all the time, so I didn't have to deal with the daily surveillance, and her husband and I were cool, so everything was great. I started my job in Rancho Cucamonga at a mortgage-collections call center. There I met new friends, new co-workers, and found a new side of myself. I had the financial stability of a good job, and I started to check in with myself about what I wanted for myself in the long run. I was happy where I was working, but I started thinking about the long game. My new best friend and work husband, Tomi, had just graduated college, and he was talking about what his next steps were. I fell in love with myself and my friends, and that was enough. Finally, I was not thinking about who was going to marry me. I was just having a good time. I was thinking about my future, and who I wanted to be in it.

By now Jason and I had stopped lying to ourselves, and each other. I was twenty-four, and I'd learned more about myself and him. I'd figured out what I wanted, and so had he. Turned out we wanted each other again. We decided to insulate ourselves, fuck what everyone else had to say. It happened so quickly, that after one phone call, we realized we were back together. It had been years of talking to each other in the background and thinking to myself about it, so all it took was one phone call of conversation.

I visited Susanville for what turned out to be the last time after we got back together. We had long conversations while looking each other in the eye, making sure we were both totally sure. It was a huge step, and we were ready to take it. Not even a month after the visit, Jason was transferred from Susanville to Calipatria State Prison, only a few hours away. Everything was working out and looking up. Visiting was much easier, so the letters were rarer, but we still used them to talk regularly.

2005
Dear big homie, =)

Hi, babe. =) How are you and the kids doing? I hope all of you are in the best of health, mind, and spirit. Miss you guys!!!!!!! I'm super, super sick. I actually have a tissue stuck up my nose while I'm writing this letter. I've been sick for the last couple days, but I wanted to write you.

I want to thank you for my card. You always send me bomb cards, but this one was my favorite.

Are you sure you can put up with me for a lifetime? =)

I'm gonna have to send you the consent forms that need to get notarized. Let me know how much it is, and I'll get you the money.

I see while you were writing me your picture arrived. Talking about how "I knew you would see things my way." Keeonna, I always see things your damn way. Haven't you figured that out yet? It hasn't always been like that. I wouldn't be in prison if it were. But I'm learning. =)

Anyway, I'm glad you got your picture. Don't let your sancho get ahold of this one. =) Honestly, I know I don't have to worry about another cat coming into your life, because Tre and Eamon aren't having it. =) When you get time write me back. As soon as possible.

Keep your head up and be safe out there. Good luck with school.

With all my love,
With all my life,
Jason

PS
Hurry up and write back! =)
When we get married, names are changing, damn it.

2005
Dear Jason,

Hey, babe. I hope you're feeling better. I'm glad you liked your cards; I knew that would cheer you up. Tre and Eamon are good.

School is going really well. I've discovered that I love math! I think I'm gonna add math as a second major. Mr. Mayne is the best math teacher ever. He even teaches Tre and Eamon. I always thought I was bad at it.

I told Mom we was getting married. She didn't pay me no attention. I think she didn't believe me. Oh well. She'll see when the day comes. As soon as I get the papers, I'll get them notarized so we can start planning to get married.

This letter will be a short one because I gotta finish my homework and check on the boys. I gotta make sure they did

they homework and get ready for work. Don't be a crybaby.
I'll write you again tomorrow.

Love,

KeKe

Things fell into place. Jason was three hours away. I had a
good job at Freemont Investment as a loan counselor. The kids
were older, so I didn't have to drag toddlers or babies with me to a
visit. Tre was ten and Eamon seven, and they got dressed on their
own. Eamon was with his dad on the weekends, but Tre was independent enough that when we did get ready for Calipatria, he put
himself together and entertained himself on the drive.

I checked out the website for Calipatria before our first visit.
Before we could create our vision for family, before we had the
chance to fully grow up, before we figured out how to make a
home instead of just playing house, before we could see home in
each other, I had to reconsider what I knew home to be. With me
and Jason being closer than ever, I thought I was ready for us to
start our life together as adults. All I needed to do was figure out
the right steps.

At the time Calipatria was a new prison, so there were new
rules and new procedures I had to prepare for. Susanville was so
far away, there weren't a lot of visitors. The few times I was there
it was easy. Calipatria's closer to LA, and it's where most people
from LA get locked up. At first I didn't know how strict this prison
was or how crowded. When I traveled out the way to Susanville,
COs cut me some slack sometimes, just because they knew how
far I had to go to visit. For Calipatria I couldn't expect the same
grace. Jason had been at Susanville for two years before my first

visit, so he could relay messages through the whisper network of the prison about what it was like, how to visit, how to act, who to talk to. But by the time he landed in Calipatria, he was new. He was in Receiving and Release for the first month, the limbo space before you get assigned to a cell or placed in the prison. You get assigned to R&R when you first come to the prison or when you're getting ready to go home. No information got to me because they don't allow phone calls in R&R, only letters, and by the time he found something out and wrote me a letter, shit may have changed, or he would be assigned to a yard and able to call. I had to do my own research and make a list of what I needed to go visit. I could read every guide and list, every step I needed to take to visit, check every box, but I couldn't know how Calipatria really worked until I could see and learn for myself what visitation was like. Research on the prison space couldn't ready my heart space. Unwritten rules in love, in heart, in life, have to be learned and unlearned. I was trying to make a new home with Jason, to take the next step like I had moved on from the past. Our past together, my past with my dad, my mom, my granny. Me and Jason were going to make a home together, even if we had to bring the prison along with us. Nothing about this shit is practical. There's no rhyme or reason. The steps are bullshit. Navigating prison is bullshit. All of it is learned on the fly.

SQUARE BIZ

Before we were boxed in. Before they started taking folks I'd known my whole life and put them in new boxes, prisons, or caskets. Our box was supposed to be home. You know, like that Stephanie Mills song in *The Wiz*: "When I think of home, I think of a place where there's love overflowing." Our box was a place of uplift and security, but it ended up a place where there was one way in and one way out for all of us. Where I'm from, one of the first questions people ask is "Where you from?" You claim a place, and a place has to claim you back. That house, I didn't live there until I was nineteen, but I always did. My mail never went there, but I always did. After school, winter break, spring break, summer, that's where I felt comfortable and safe. It will always belong to me, regardless of what the deed says.

I was raised in a box. I mean, not literally, but seriously. My mom and I always lived in apartments, little boxes stacked together in units and complexes on different street grids in Los Angeles, California. But these apartments were never home. Our apartments were always a place to sleep. They never belonged to us, and I never felt like I belonged there. My mom loved everything clean, so our house was like a museum of cleanliness. It was pretty, orderly, well-maintained, for anyone who would come visit. But when you lived in that house, there was no comfort. My mom worked all the time, so we were never there. Our couch had to last, so we couldn't sit on it. We never ate meals at our table. My mom wanted to make sure the space would last, and she was always worried about something breaking or having to replace something. You want to watch TV? Sit on the floor, but don't mess up the clear vacuum lines that she made sure stayed in the carpet. You hungry? Stand in the kitchen and eat; be sure to clean up after yourself. Our mail went to our apartment, which was listed as our address for everything, but it was never home.

Home will always be my granny's house on Courtney Street, built as part of a walled community called Franklin Squares in Watts, California. Granny's house was boxed in by concrete and asphalt and an off-white brick wall welcoming you to Courtney Street, a road leading to two cul-de-sacs. One way in and one way out. When she first moved into the house in 1979, it was yellow. But I never knew that until I looked at old photos. Franklin Squares was built as part of a planned community by Ted Watkins, a Black community organizer and businessman who moved to Watts from Mississippi when he was thirteen. In the 1970s Franklin Squares was supposed to be part of the revitalization of Watts, to beautify an area that was still recovering from the Watts Riots in 1965. White police officers had pulled over a young Black man, Marquette Frye, for a DUI, but refused to release his car to his mother, Rena Price, or brother, Ronald, at the scene. An argument broke out, a fight broke out, a crowd gathered, and Rena, Marquette, and Ronald all got arrested. Six days of insurgency, protest, violence, and unrest followed as people spoke back against the brutality, racism, and policing that infected the community. So when Ted Watkins bought the area that became Franklin Squares, it was part of the call for better housing and services to transform the image of Watts.

When I tell people that I'm from Watts, they usually say, "Oh, like in *Menace II Society*." The word "Watts" rings out in LA culture, period. You can't talk about LA without shouting us out. Unfortunately, we are also known for gang violence, Watts riots in 1965 and 1992, and the crack epidemic. Most folks can't reconcile the story versus the reality of Watts. The story of Watts begins in many places. The area that we know as Watts is the homeland of the Gabrielino/Tongva peoples, colonized by Spain, and designated Rancho La Tajauta in an 1843 Mexican land grant. The United States took over the conquest and colonization after the Mexican-American War and Treaty of Guadalupe Hildago in 1848. In the 1870s the United States was trying to encourage western expansion into the new state of California, selling and subdividing parcels of land, including the 220-acre parcel sold to Charles H. Watts in 1886.

The arrival of the railroads brought growth and further development of the area. Before the 1940s people called Watts Mud Town because there were so few city services and so many Black people. No roads, no bricks—it was viewed as a transplant of the Deep South, country-living with a growing Black population migrating from the South, the majority of whom were employed as Pullman car porters. World War II brought the second greatest migration of Black people leaving the Southern states, headed for success and a new beginning in California, working in the war industries. During that time there was a population boom as more and more Black folks settled in Watts; meanwhile, the white people moved out. Because of the influx of Black workers, three housing communities were built: the Jordan Downs, Imperial Courts, and the Nickerson Gardens. Just a few years later you would see a big shift between homeowners and renters. Black folks who would be categorized as having decent jobs started to purchase small homes within the community; on the other side of that spectrum, poor Black folks continued to live in the projects, which had become subsidized housing in the 1950s. Ted Watkins was part of that migration from the South and built the Franklin Squares as the answer to the public perception of Watts. Building up the area would mean jobs, hiring people from the area to build the houses, and neighborhood cleanups through the Watts Labor Community Action Committee (WLCAC). Before the Squares, my granny, mom, and aunie started in the Jordan Downs projects and lived in a small apartment just two blocks from the house we would all call home. My mom and aunie's first jobs were painting buildings and picking up trash for the WLCAC. Not knowing that a few years later we would be in the Squares, we were always thankful for the WLCAC, not just for giving my mom and aunie jobs but for giving my granny the house.

Granny's house is a lucky house. She won it in a housing lottery by the WLCAC for low-income folks in 1979 at Will Rogers Park (which is now named after Ted Watkins). Granny told me she thought it was fake but went to the park anyway. The lottery was on April 1, April Fools' Day, but the chance at a real house was too big to pass on. You had to be in the park the day of the lottery, so 1,600 people gathered in the park with Ted Watkins, Mayor

Tom Bradley, and Governor Jerry Brown to win thirty-nine houses. Granny always told me she was the second-to-last name drawn.

It was a green stucco box near the corner. I loved Granny's house, and not just because it was the same color as the green in the Baskin-Robbins' rainbow sherbet. Granny's house was always immaculate, inside and out. When you look good, people don't ask questions. Her front yard was precisely manicured, wrapped in pink flowers—Fuchsia Glow Hydrangea and Peppermint Roses. Granny's flowers weren't the kind you saw in the store or got on Valentine's Day. They were a vibrant, big situation that was perfectly kept and maintained. The front door was a heavy wood that would take your finger off if it got caught in it. The front yard took up the whole front of the house, and the front door was hidden off to the side next to the driveway and the two-car-garage. In her later years at the house, she didn't even park in the garage; she kept a private little fridge there with a TV and Jacuzzi so she could live in luxury without having to drive all the way out to Jack LaLanne Fitness Club near downtown after doing a run over at Will Rogers Park. She used to sit in the Jacuzzi with all the lights off, with the door an inch off the ground to let in some air. That garage became her church, to praise and thank God, to cry and grieve, and her escape from us.

Stepping into the front door of Granny's house was like walking by the perfume counter at a department store: grown-woman perfume that just lived in the house with my granny. You could always tell the day of the week and my granny's mood by the smell of her perfume. If it was a deep, warm, spicy smell—that sanctified, respectable, classy smell that matched her God-fearing burgundy-reddish lipstick—it was time for church. If she was going out, had a boyfriend, or was married at the time, the perfume smelled like attention, a flirty-fun, heavily floral smell like romance was in the air. But on a regular day-to-day basis, her house smelled like flowers or evaporated milk or syrup, lightly floral with strong sweetness—like the butterscotch candies she kept in her purse but never really ate. This perfume was like her work uniform, an everyday kind of smell that blended with the smell of food she had cooked at some point during the day—eggs cooked in browned butter, oatmeal, or pancakes.

Granny kept a tall mirror near the front door, big enough to see yourself from the knees up. That way you could always check yourself going in or going out to make sure you looked right. To the left were the built-in wooden shelves with trophies from my ballet, tap, and drill teams or Kawai's bowling league. My cousins' and my accomplishments went up in Granny's house, never in the homes we lived in; they were Granny's accomplishments just as much as they were ours. To the right of the trophies were where our most current school pictures resided. My granny always got the biggest picture out of the school picture package to put on her wall. Inside the doorway was the coat closet that always smelled old and stale like mothballs, probably because we never used it and the only things in there were a few leather jackets that hadn't been worn since the seventies. Of course, the doors to the coat closet were also floor-to-ceiling mirrors, so you always had a chance to look at yourself. My mom and I always lived in some little two-bedroom apartment where everything was close together, so Granny's house felt like a mansion. Everybody could fit when the family came over: me, my mom, my aunie, Kawai, Antwoine, Granny, and her husband (if she was married at the time).

I'd always wanted to have a seat at the table. For me, sitting at the table meant I had made it. I had moved up the hierarchical ladder of my family. It meant I was up there with Granny; it solid-ified my place as her best friend, confidant, and favorite. It let ev-eryone in the family know beyond a shadow of a doubt that I had a place, and my spot couldn't be taken—unspoken law. The deep chestnut color, the pronounced wood-grained marbling, and the shiny coat of lacquer was a sight to see; it was magical. My granny would always say that her table was for special occasions or grown folks. But neither was true because I ain't never seen anybody sit at that table, not even her. She would always tell this story about the time she noticed there was a hole in her white lace tablecloth. She lined all us children up—Antwoine, Kawai, and myself—and asked who made the hole. She said, laughing, "Kee said, 'Now, Granny, you know we ain't messed with that table.'" She just laughed and laughed because she knew it was the truth.

When I got the chance to sit in that olive-green velvet-cushioned chair, I felt like royalty. But that feeling didn't last long. I surely never thought that my first time having sex would set off a chain of firsts that would change the direction of my life. The first time I sat at my granny's table was when I was two months pregnant with Tre. We were a Good Black Christian Family™, and my granny went to *church*. Me being pregnant was blowing up our whole spot. The appearance of our Good Black Christian Family™ was going to be ruined with this pregnant teenage girl. We had to make it right as a family because we went to church as a family, we went to Bible school as a family. Now fifteen-year-old Keeonna put ev-erything into question (never mind that Antwoine had Antwoine Jr. a year before and nobody had said a word). We had to sit at the table as a family and figure this out. So the heads of the fam-ily sat at the table: my mom, my granny, and Granny's pastor. He was part of our extended family. Granny brought the pastor to the table to amplify her opinions (I needed to keep this baby, because abortion was wrong and God hated the sin and not the sinner) but also to keep our standing in the church and the eyes of the pastor. My granny sat me at the table, but more like a job interview or interrogation. They sat me at the head of the table across from Granny, the pastor, and my mother.

None of my firsts was how I imagined.

The first time sitting at the table.

The first time I felt worthless.

The first time I felt my mother's love fade.

The first time I understood that I was a disappointment.

The first time my granny looked at me differently.

The first time I saw sadness in my mother's eyes when she looked at me.

The first time I understood my place in the family.

The first time I understood what my family thought of me.

The first time I thought that God didn't love me anymore.

The first time I felt betrayed by my body.

The first time I clearly saw my family.

My mom sat with her head tilted to the side, eyes wide open, tight-lipped and looking at all of us upside the head in between her fussing back and forth with my granny and the pastor. My granny sat there, looking at me and smiling every now again between all the fussing. I learned quickly what was behind her smile. I had been initiated into the bad daughters' club, where we are bonded by shame. She sat there with a smile and looked very proud of herself; she was happy. My granny always needed to be the center of attention or somebody's hero; my pregnancy gave her the opportunity to do both. She now had a partner in crime, someone she could share her own shame with. It was never for my own good; she needed to be needed. But that didn't last long.

A seat at the table was a monumental coming-of-age moment, but it also shifted my perspective of myself and my family. What I didn't quite understand at the time was that sitting in that chair didn't give me the freedom I thought I would gain but in fact put me in a box labeled "Teen Mom." This point in my life seemed like a competition between me, Kawai, and Antwoine. We didn't even know we were competing against one another. But our family had placed their bets long ago on who would be the one—the successful one. They invested so much in us to succeed, but when I got pregnant, I saw my odds change. Like in the movies about the stock market: you see all the stockbrokers going crazy to buy what's hot, and next thing you know, that stock ain't worth a dime. My stock dipped. Nobody wanted it anymore, so my family started placing other bets. Was I still good, could I still play and compete, or should I forfeit? These were the questions that constantly played in my head.

If being pregnant wasn't already embarrassing, shameful, and lonely, I was being ripped away from the two people who meant the most to me at the time: my cousins Kawai and Antwoine. In 1995 we were now all traveling down different roads. Kawai was becoming a highly sought-after basketball star and had moved to Los Angeles with her parents, who had just bought a house off Normandie and Vermont. Antwoine had moved out and started his own family but was straddling the fence of being a street nigga and being the man my granny wanted him to be. Before that time we had never been separated. We had lived together and went to the same schools; we did everything together. Now the distance was loud. We were separated by the 605 and newly built 105 freeway, long-distance calls, travel ball, college scouts, and my growing stomach. Kawai didn't have time for me anymore; she kept soaring, and I was in the bleachers with the rest of my family, watching. Her days were now filled with regular high school shit—games, friends, winter formals, homecoming, prom, and college tours. Shit that I was supposed to be doing too. Instead, I was going to prenatal appointments, adjusting to a new high school for pregnant moms, navigating a new silence between me and my mother, and trying to figure out my new normal.

I decided I wasn't out of the game just yet, and therefore my people-pleasing and overachiever attitude was born. I am always eager to please. In my family, if you were smart and wanted to survive the ups and downs of whichever adult was going through something—and there was always somebody going through something—you learned to read: read body language, read lips, read what was being said without words. I realized I had mastered reading my mom by age eight when she stopped setting reminders—she didn't have to tell me to clean the house, to keep my grades up, how to talk to adults, and how to act when she was looking and when she was not. When my mom stopped fussing and I didn't get in trouble, I knew that she thought she knew who I was, so I could fly under the radar and do what I wanted as long as she got the actions and attitude that she wanted. When I was a little girl, I wanted to make my mom and Granny happy, so I always did what they wanted me to do. Seeing their smiling faces meant love, but more importantly, it kept me safe. Being pregnant blew up my world; my cover was blown, and I was exposed. Until my pregnancy, my family hadn't a clue as to who I was. My mom knew that I listened to her, I got good grades, I had plans for my future. But they didn't know me; they didn't see me. So now that my secret was growing in my belly, I had to learn to reinvent myself, learn to please folks all over again. But this time it wasn't for love; it was to prove my worth as a member of my family and to prove to myself that I was still good, still KeKe, still capable of following through with the original plans I had for my life. To stay in the game, I had to go for broke.

Once they broke up the team of me, Kawai, and Antwoine, they put us in competition with one another, and I had to show up and show out. I was up against Kawai, Ms. #24, the showstopper; people was calling her Kobe even before he stole her number. She had the potential to be the successful one in our family because she was a basketball star gifted with academics, on a clear path to college. She was set up for success. Next up was Antwoine, Mr. Real Boss Player, the player who taught Kawai how to play, who took sports serious—but not serious enough to keep him out of the streets. He showed Kawai how to be a star but fucked up his own path to college, straddling the fence between the streets and school. He got his girlfriend pregnant at eighteen, went to prison for ten years at twenty-one, but he was the oldest and only boy in our family. No matter what he did wrong, he could do no wrong. He might not be the brightest star in the sky, but he will always be talked about and centered in our family. That just left me, Keeonna, Ms. Mom, the girl who *was*. Bumped from the varsity starting lineup to coming off the bench for the JV team. Before I was pregnant, I was the performer, a cute little doll that could do pageants, that my family could pick up to play with and entertain, and put down and not worry about. But once I got pregnant, the Keeonna they thought they knew was gone. The image of Keeonna changed in their eyes and could never go back.

In my family, image is everything. All of our moments, for good or bad, were captured in real time in our photos that Granny put right by the front door of her house on Courtney Street. The first thing you saw when you walked in the door was the pictures. Once you came in the door, you had to take off your shoes, but while you were taking off your shoes, Granny lined up her pictures just the way she wanted. There was space for the graduation portraits of me, Kawai, and Antwoine to sit side by side on the wall. Antwoine was the oldest boy, so he got the top spot on the wall. A picture of just himself, a silk shirt underneath his cap and gown, with little cuts in his eyebrows, holding his diploma high to show off the fancy class ring Granny bought him, with a serious face and little smise, because he knew he was handsome and poppin'. Me and Kawai graduated at the same time, but her photo was next in line, by itself. Kawai had a fresh flat iron—one of the only times she ever had long hair—wearing her mom's green silk shirt that Kawai loved to match with the green and gold of her high school, with a white cap and gown. Inset and feathered in the corner was a small picture-in-picture of Kawai, still wearing the green silk shirt but without the cap and gown, holding her basketball. And on the bottom was my graduation picture. I wore the same white cap and gown as Kawai, with a rose-colored silk shirt underneath, with my granny's borrowed heart locket necklace she made me wear because she said I needed a little gold or something as well. My hair was long and flat-ironed. But for my picture-in-picture there was my one-year-old baby, Tre, in a little army-green-and-tan-striped cardigan, with matching shirt and pants. My pride and shame on full display in one picture—the graduation picture showed all of me, just as a mom. I wanted him in the picture because he's my baby, but seeing it on the wall in the family hierarchy meant something else. It was a constant reminder to my granny, her church friends, and everyone who came to visit of how Keeonna fell from grace and was now just a mom. My baby was my pride and joy, and I wanted him in my picture, but I also knew that my picture was just one more way of boxing me in. The little box frame on Granny's wall was a way of showing my granny's favorite saying: "Boys and books don't mix." I was graduated, but instead of heading off to college like Kawai, I was expected to just work and be a mom.

Since my family's expectations had changed, I knew I had to set new expectations for myself. Nobody was talking about me going to college anymore; I was rerouted into what my family thought was a good, stable job: working customer service for a phone company. My aunie got me the job right out of high school, because it was good, respectable work that I could do until I retired, pay for my kids, and live life. This checked every box that my family now expected: raise kids, have money, be a mom. This was not the hype and expectations my family had given me as a kid. I was set up to be a star with my mom: in beauty pageants, going to Spelman, becoming a doctor—dreams I had told my family and they had supported wholeheartedly. Now that I had a baby I wasn't supposed to shoot for the stars; I was kept grounded to set up a good foundation.

Now I was part of a tradition of dreams being boxed up and saved for conversations, not something to be lived. My granny had kids young and looked for jobs to sustain her family, not following her own dreams—she never even told me what she wanted to be before she became a mom. She just knew she had to be a young mom, and her future was getting a husband, not getting work. She learned that you couldn't depend on a man to sustain your family, so she made taking care of yourself and your kids the priority for all her girls to come—your own money, your own situation. My mom had me while she was premed, but then her dreams of being a doctor got boxed up for nursing school so she could make sure we wouldn't need my dad for a damn thing. My aunie had Kawai young but never wanted to go to college anyway, so she went to the phone company, where she worked for thirty years until she retired. Now I was at the same phone company, with a job that I was supposed to work until I retired.

But I knew I wasn't supposed to settle for less; my mom taught me I was the one and never the two. I couldn't just go work at the phone company; that didn't match the dreams of grandeur I had, that my mom had. Everyone in our family had raised us well, but everyone always pushed us to be better. Even though they told me to be regular when I got pregnant, I knew I wasn't regular from everything they had told me before. My family talked about reaching for the stars, moving together as a unit, supporting one another with whatever we brought to the table. They talked about being better, but when I made choices that didn't match what they wanted, they put me right back to what they were comfortable with, what they knew and expected. They thought there was safety in the box because it was something that we knew and understood. The box of the house and the neighborhood led me to more boxes that I had to fight my way out of. The pregnancy test came in a box. The security booth where I got caught stealing the pregnancy test was a box holding me. The positive on the pregnancy test was a little box that took me finally to Granny's table in her little house in the Squares, where my family decided my future for me. And Granny put me up in the lowest frame on her wall, sharing the box with my baby. It wasn't until I started visiting Jason in prison that I realized how to break out of the box and how to come together with a family, not the ones I was born with but the ones who offered me a seat, a whole table, and anything they had to share because they knew I would do the same.

SPREAD

I love noodles, and not that Cup Noodles shit. I'm very particular; I only eat Maruchan ramen: creamy chicken or chicken
flavor. I don't know where all this talk of "This a poor man's
meal" came from. I can do some amazing shit with a pack of
noodles. My mom worked a lot, so noodles were my go-to meal,
and they got better every time I made them. Our cabinets were
filled with food that would last, that had a long shelf life, that
was canned, and food that I could make for her and me to enjoy.
I'm not like my cousins, who would just eat cereal for dinner;
I wanted a meal. Something that was hot and tasted good and
that made me sleep good. My mom was dead tired when she got
home, so I was the cook. Plus my mom couldn't cook to save her
life. I still can't figure out how she is my granny's child and can't
scramble eggs. At first I was just adding water and the contents of
the shiny foil packet. But the scientist in me couldn't stop there. I

perfected the water-to-noodle ratio because I don't like too much broth in my bowl, then I figured out the precise time to turn off the burner, which made the texture of the noodles exquisite. I made noodles at least once a week, which meant I experimented with a new ingredient each time. At first I was cautious, adding in hot sauce and garlic powder. Then I moved up, started adding Lawry's Seasoned Salt, pepper, garlic powder, onion powder, thyme, the seasoning packet, and hitting it with some sprinkles of Tapatío when I was ready to eat. The way each noodle would coil between the tines of my fork, wrapped around like little vines in "Jack and the Beanstalk," to form the perfect bite each time. Ramen gets taken for granted, but when you pull the ingredients together in the right way? Magic.

I learned my magic from my granny, how to throw the ingredients together and turn something that people take for granted into a whole meal, a magic of flavors. When I got pregnant with Tre, I felt like I had lost my coven and my own magic. I started second-guessing myself and all the recipes for success that I had been taught. My pregnancy strained the connections with my mom and Granny because they didn't see me as this mystical, magical being capable of fantastical things. I had become plain and ordinary, with no spark. Granny conjured and manifested what she wanted and talked about us as these magical beings through her awe-inspired disbelief at our accomplishments. When I got pregnant her awe turned into a matter-of-fact resignation. "I can't believe she can do that" turned into "I can't believe she did that." I still made ramen, and I still cooked like my granny taught me, but I had to pull together the ingredients for myself. I didn't find myself and my magic again until I was hundreds of miles away from home.

• • •

I first met Chastity in 2005, on my first visit to Calipatria State Prison all by myself. When I look back now, it's obvious how out of place I was. On my first weekend visit, I thought everything would work like it did in the regular world: visitation started at eight a.m., so as long as I got to the prison by six a.m., everything would be cool. But then I pulled up two hours early to the disaster-movie line, and there was no way all of these people just happened to show up at 5:59. By the time I got to the front, I was number two hundred and something. I had to wait to get into the gates of the prison, and then another two hours waiting to get my number called to go through security and go to the visiting room at Jason's yard. By the time I got to the actual yard, it was a little after ten thirty.

Jason was on a yard with not many visits that day, so I was able to study and read each person in the visiting room once we got in. I hadn't seen any of these women in the line, and they were already in the middle of their visits when I walked in the room. I was sitting in a chair by the vending machines and the plain walls, with the CO watching the cameras and all of us sitting inside. Visiting was light, so the three other couples in the room were spread to the corners. After waiting for almost five hours, I still in my head thought that we would at least have a few hours of time to ourselves—it was almost eleven, and visitation ended at three. Once Jason finally came in, we started talking about how different visitation was at Calipat. At the first prison, when Jason was in High Desert, it was so far away that I was rarely able to make the fourteen-hour drive, and nobody else was really there, so the line was maybe three or four people who had moved to the town to live and visit regularly.

Even though Calipatria was closer, visiting was going to have to work differently. He was ready for me at 8:10 because he was expecting it to be like High Desert too—once it got to be around ten, he just thought I wasn't coming. We had to figure something out to make this work, so Jason offered to talk to some other men on the yard. "I'll talk to ol' boy, I know him from families, and we'll figure out what's up." I believed him, and I appreciated him putting in the work, but you can't trust a man to do a woman's job. How did I know he was gonna ask the right questions or get the answers we need? So me being me, I made plans to go and talk to one of the other women when visitation was done. Even though they said visitation ended at three p.m., they were kicking everybody out by 2:40 to make sure they could get everyone back to count and all the visitors out of the prison by three p.m.

Once visitation was done, the guards yelled out, "VISTATION IS OVER. SAY YOUR GOODBYES. MEN, AGAINST THE WALL; VISTORS, STAND BY THIS WALL." They lined up the men on one end of the room and the visitors by the exit, counted off the incarcerated men, and sent them through the door and locked it up. Only then would they open up the exit for visitors and call out our names to collect our IDs and visitation slips before they let us out the prison. As I was waiting in line for them to call our names and let us out, I approached the woman in front of me. "Hi, my name's Keeonna. I didn't see you in the line outside; how did you get to be in here?" She was super dressed up, like she was going somewhere. She had a maxi skirt, fitted baby tee, a little jacket, and three-inch stilettos. Her hair was in a bomb deep-wave weave; she had full makeup, perfume. She looked like she was going on a date to a fine restaurant—somewhere she could go out and be seen. I was there in my tracksuit, trying to be comfortable. I didn't know the dress code; I was trying to stay safe. Don't get it twisted; it was a burgundy velour tracksuit with my tennis shoes, comfortable but nice. She told me her name was Chastity, and she got in early "because I live here." She asked if I was coming next weekend, and I of course said yes. Chastity gave me her number and told me to call her during the week, and that was that. That next Thursday I called up Chastity like she said, and let her know I was coming to visit that weekend. "Can I meet you at your house and go in with you?" Chastity simply said, "Yeah," and gave me her address. "My dude, Anthony, told me he talked to your dude, so I'm gonna show you. Meet me at the house between 7:15 and 7:20, and we can ride in your car to the prison." When I met with Chastity that weekend, the real training began.

● ● ●

In my head I figured we would just show up early and go to the prison; she had some kind of magic recipe from just living close to the prison. I was already nervous. Chastity was talking about meeting at 7:15, and last week I showed up at six and didn't get in till ten. I was still in the blind, but something told me to trust her, so I didn't ask any questions. I pulled up to Chastity's house—a small, little studio home, lined up in a row of other little units. An ugly little brown box in the middle of the desert, a flat-roof home that looked like it was made out of clay, trimmed in white, surrounded by dirt. No driveway, no sidewalk, just dirt. When I pulled up I went to the door to check in with Chastity. I knocked and Chastity came to the door, and I asked to use the bathroom, but she had a smart mouth. "No, you can use the bathroom outside." She laughed and welcomed me into the house. As I came in to use the bathroom, I saw two other women doing their finishing touches of hair and makeup. Everyone was dressing up, but not *too* fancy and *not* out of dress code. I was still casual and just looking to use the bathroom. We waved, but I wasn't sure how this was all gonna work. It was 7:15. There were no other cars outside—I had no problem giving them a ride—but I didn't think we were gonna get in on time. So I used the bathroom in peace and walked out, and Chastity immediately said, "Let's go so we won't be late."

As we all got into the car, Chastity casually introduced me to Dana and Michelle as they got in the back seat. I had to rely on Chastity to get me from her house to the prison; this was long before I could get any kind of directions on my phone. Chastity led me down the back roads, and I was just following directions on faith since I had seen her already in the room the week before. As we came to the back of the line, I slowed to stop, but Chastity told me to keep going, so I started inching past the car in front of me. "Girl, go!" Chastity said with a laugh. I kept going all the way down to the front of the line when I realized Chastity was a witch. We were the first car in line. As soon as I put the car in park, Chastity said, "You see that car right there? That's Dana's car; when she gets here on Friday, we go to the prison and park the car to hold our spot for visiting." That was the smartest shit I'd heard. What I heard through ear hustling in the processing room last time was that most women that came to visit usually got to the prison by midnight and parked their cars in the line and slept in their cars. Then they woke up, brushed their teeth, and washed their faces using water bottles. That was the usual protocol. But Chastity said, "Fuck that, we're too old to be sleeping in somebody car, and I need to look rested." Chastity had the game figured out and built something bigger than the prison in the process.

Chastity had a house. Me and Dana had cars. Michelle offered whatever money she could spare. We started a schedule to make it work; each of us would take turns driving out to Calipatria on Friday. Dana didn't work Fridays, so she could get her car to the front every time. I had to come up after work, but I had to get there by a reasonable time so we could all go into town, get food, and have a meal together. Michelle caught rides with others or would rent a car on her own to make her way there, depending on the schedule. We all offered something to make it work. We figured out the line, we made driving schedules, we made visitation work for us. Even if other women didn't like us personally, we drew a lot of attention because we were always first into processing, first into visitation. Other women would see us, and some would ask questions, and some would just watch us carefully. As they watched and tried to do shit, we had to change course. Some other groups might figure out we put a car up front and try and beat us to the front. Every now and then somebody might beat us to the front of the line, and that put us on notice. But we had the home field advantage: Chastity lived in town, and nobody could compete with that. If somebody was parking earlier on Friday, Dana would come stay at Chastity's on Thursday night to secure our spot. If Dana wasn't able to make it, Chasity got some orange traffic cones and would walk over early to secure our spot. We were the one, and never the two.

Visitation, for the state, is a "privilege." Patronizing signs posted all over the visitation rooms make it sound like the state is doing you a favor by allowing you to see your people for a few short hours on the weekend. Meanwhile, for our people on the inside, it's the biggest incentive the state has to offer. Behave, or you can't see people who love you. If people don't visit, it's because you're unlovable. It's never really about keeping the family together or giving people a glimpse of humanity in spite of the mistakes they may have made. It's about control. It's about power. The state makes it as difficult and ugly as possible. Prisons are in the middle of nowhere, hidden behind a dehumanizing series of hoops to go through just to see somebody for a few short hours. Hours of driving, if you're lucky. Gas is expensive, and you either gotta rent a room or stay in your car. Staying in a car isn't safe—it's cold and the middle of the desert; you're bringing your whole life in a bag or in a car. And don't let you have kids. You also don't know anybody who works there or visits there. People saw us well rested and dressed up to go in while they slept in their cars. Then there's the waiting. Waiting outside to get in. Waiting inside to get farther in. Waiting inside for your loved one to visit. Waiting to get back outside. Waits on waits on waits. The hoops of the hoops of the hoops. And you can't ask questions, can't handle things the way you might have, because the state and the prison are right there—one step out of line and you're inside somewhere else, rather than inside to see your loved ones.

Control is also about the illusion of choice. All these obstacles and hurdles are about tricking people into thinking that we make the decision to stop coming, when it's not. The constant hurdles and obstacles are designed to make visitors feel like it's not worth it. The prison benefits from us visiting; we get to be the carrot they dangle out for people inside. But the prison also doesn't want us there—they make it clear with the hoops, hurdles, and obstacles. If we come, the state benefits. If we don't come, now the state benefits by blaming the people inside, blaming people outside—everyone's to blame but the prison.

So when I tell you Chastity is a sorcerer, believe me. She brought us together and harmonized our gifts. We finessed the line; we finessed the system. We built relationships with one another, and then we started finessing the COs. We got to know all the guards, everybody on the yards. Chastity could talk her way in and out of everything. She was Danny Ocean. She had the whole situation planned and mapped. Each week was practice for the next. I was nice, and young, and I still had a sweet baby face. I knew how to talk my way into what I wanted. We used everything we had to make it work. I had the most formal education, so I knew how to read the rules of the prison. Prison is good about giving rules, but in the middle of all the things you can't do, there's a lot of things that you can. I was Chastity's right hand, her main backup, and her advisor—jumping in to play good cop if things didn't go the way Chastity wanted. Dana looked like a church lady. She wore stockings still, for crying out loud. She was our contortionist and master of disguise. We could put Dana in any position, but she was so sweet, nobody would believe she could do anything wrong. So we could get away with more, because why would Dana do anything bad? Michelle was our cover. She was six foot tall and built. She was like a giant Peg Bundy—no spandex pants because it was outta dress code—but her hair was big like Dolly Parton's. If somebody was outta dress code, somebody was bringing in more money than allowed. She took up space, drew attention, and knew how to talk to people. She was critical for the COs because she knew how to talk and when to talk. She was on the mind of every CO when she walked in the door just because of how she looked, but she could carry on a conversation. Michelle also had some health problems with her hip, not enough to be a real obstacle to her but enough that she knew how to ask for help, how to work the room. We used everything we had to our benefit. You have to fight the state a little differently to outsmart them.

We were beating the state at its own game. As much as prison is about cells and division, it's more about keeping people away from one another and grinding you into nothingness. We created a collective where we found real connection and joy. We figured out happiness on those weekends. That's what we looked forward to. And not because of these men, but we had such a good time with one another, together. We found friendship and joy and love that made the process seamless. It wasn't even a thought of how to visit. Prisons are about punishing a person and everyone they're connected to. When you take someone away from society to learn their so-called lesson, you're punishing anyone who might have ever cared about them. So when we kept going, we got married, had kids, did everything that was supposed to stop once the prison got involved. But we kept going and did what we wanted anyway. It wasn't easy, but we took what we had and we made it work.

Sometimes you have to use the bullshit that life gives you and make it into something beautiful. Even though we'd been given the worst parts of things, we could make it into something amazing. We built our weekly visits to a terrible place into something beautiful. The same happened inside. When you're around other people, you start to build community in the ways you can for survival. In prison, people will come together for a big meal, throwing everything they have into a spread. Some people inside are lucky enough to have family order them a little hot plate to heat up food in their cell. Not everybody's family can afford to send a package, but this cheap little burner is a big deal. But others might have commissary foods that they can throw in. If you don't have family that can send you food, you might work in the kitchen and be able to get some ingredients to throw in. Chicken could be a come-up. But maybe you work in laundry and can help with the cleanup or take clothes for others next time. Everyone has something to offer, and when we throw in together, we can make something better. So everybody puts in their contribution. Top Ramen. Cheese Whiz. Cut-up summer sausage. Corn chips. Doritos (if you want to up your nacho flavor). Braiding hair. How to draw and make a card. So then everybody throws in, and you make a spread that might not sound like the best, most gourmet or even nutritious meal. But everybody pitches in something to make it better. It turns a bunch of junk food into a meaningful meal, because everybody plays a part and everybody makes it together. And while people on the inside are making their spread on the weekdays, we build our spread on the weekends in the visits.

● ● ●

We started out as a quartet, but our band was ready to expand. Our crew of regulars started with me, Chastity, Dana, and Michelle, but we started to branch out and be cool with other cliques of women who visited. Two other women who were regulars to visitation like us moved into the duplexes where Chastity lived. We didn't keep our techniques of visitation a secret, and we started working with other people. There's a temptation when building community in resistance to oppression to keep it to yourselves. Your resources are scarce, and you worry about the state's backlash. If we told everybody what we were up to, maybe it wouldn't be as easy, maybe we wouldn't be able to pull off our schemes—even Chastity's magic had limits. As great as it is to make a spread, you can't share everything with everybody. We don't know everybody, so we don't know where everyone's alliances are. You don't know who's really working against you when they're working with you. You have to vet people. We never sat down to talk about exactly how and why we would vet people; it happened organically. We saw the two other women move into the duplex, and Chastity got to know them well because they would come up early and see each other in the stores. As you get to know people, it works out for the better, and now we got more friends. Now if Dana couldn't come on time, Jazzy could put her car in the line. Jazzy was a white woman, but she was born and raised around Black people, from the Bay, with a bob cut and her Cuban links. I couldn't remember the other woman's name, but we could call her Niecy. She was also Black and had a gang of kids. The duplexes became a place where people stayed because they were connected to the prison somehow. We understood what it was to live there and be in the town; nobody was here because of the schools or just for fun.

But when our group expanded, Chastity expanded her house too; she went from a studio to a one-bedroom unit. In Chastity's studio people would have to bring their own air mattresses and pile on top of one another. But with a bigger space it made it easier for Chastity to have her own space. Now I could bring Tre with me. Danielle joined our group, and she had a baby too, and now she could bring her kids. With a kitchen and a bedroom and a living room, now we could make our own food and weren't dependent on the town to go eat out. Danielle didn't come all the time, but when she came once a month with her baby now, we had space. Angela also had a son, but she was more of a monthly regular too. The world was too small in our connections to prison. I came to know Danielle because Chastity's boyfriend, Anthony, the same one who knew Jason and made sure me and Chastity connected, knew Danielle's man on the inside and brought her into the fold. At the time both Danielle and I were undergrads at Cal State, San Bernardino. Out of a campus of almost 16,000, two of us just so happened to have the fathers of our children locked up in the same prison, Calipatria State Prison.

At the time Danielle was in her early twenties, and to the rest of us in our late twenties and early thirties, Danielle was a baby, and we wanted to help take care of her. We saw her maneuvering alone, and Anthony saw Danielle's man inside as a young dude trying to figure it out and brought him into the fold. Anthony was our man on the inside who could vet and green-light everybody. If a girl was messy or a man didn't have his stuff together, everybody could get caught up in a bad situation. If somebody was gangbanging and going to pull everybody into some bullshit, Anthony was the one to catch it before it happened. Anthony was the one who brought us all together, our lookout and our bouncer, but still not our leader. He wasn't bossing us around or taking charge; he was the man at the gate to make sure nothing bad came in and nothing went wrong on the inside. But once you were in the group, Anthony wasn't telling us what to do. He was an asset, not a liability. He didn't play the boss or control games; he just brought us together and let us figure out our own path.

Our family didn't follow any traditional structure. Anthony surely wasn't playing the patriarch trying to control everything within our group. We were mostly only physically together over the weekends, but we supported one another throughout our whole lives and whole selves. A weekly visit turned into daily check-ins to see what was going on, because we were the only people we could be complete with. Even though we became friends to support our mutual needs, there was nothing transactional about our relationships. Somebody needed a ride, somebody needed to borrow money, somebody was sick or whatever—we were there for one another.

Dana was the first to get married, which was a whole group project. First the person incarcerated has to apply with their counselor for a marriage. Then the counselor approves and has to send the person on the outside an application. You have to sign off that you really want to get married. That you know what the other person is actually incarcerated for. You have to know how long they are incarcerated for. Very formal ways of asking, "Bitch, you want to do this? You for real?" Once you send that back to say you understand and you are not entering a marriage blindly or under duress, you have to go to the county clerk of the county where the prison is to apply for a marriage license. The county clerk then coordinates with the local justice of the peace to figure out the next available date for you. Once they tell you your date, you have to accept and send in all the paperwork to make sure you have your license ready for the day of your wedding. A typical wedding is friends, family, a date and venue of your choice. But the choice to get married in prison is a choice that comes with a series of decisions made for you. Dana's family didn't take her marriage seriously. She didn't invite her family because they weren't going to come anyway. Her parents were as old, churchy, and traditional as she dressed. But we were her family too, and we all showed up. The same went for Angela when she got married. Angela was like Danielle, a twice-a-month visitor with a kid, but a couple years older than me, coming up from San Diego. Her family didn't support her relationship and marriage, so we showed up for her when she needed us to. We all threw in what we had.

The weekend of the weddings was a huge celebration for us, but nowhere near traditional. Dana's and Angela's weddings were on different yards, but they wouldn't expect us to cancel out our visits for the day to go to their yards. So the weekend outside the prison was all for celebration. We helped them get everything they needed—makeup, outfit, hair, anything that might be needed to get ready. Chastity did Dana's and Angela's hair before their weddings. But because we weren't going to the little ten-minute ceremony, we were all going to celebrate at Golden Corral in town afterward, on us. We took pictures before and after the visit. We were bridesmaids who just couldn't attend the ceremony. It was important for us to celebrate one another because we were regulars who understood one another. In daily life our little celebrations weren't accepted. People were quick and vocal to tell you how displeased they were with your decisions when you visited your incarcerated loved one on a regular basis. "You're being used." "You're crazy." "That's fake." We felt seen, heard, and validated with one another, and we made sure to make one another feel those ways because we didn't get it at home.

There was a weird hierarchy of acceptance in our families. Danielle was already married when her partner got incarcerated, and he was in for a relatively short time, maybe three years. It was easier for her family to understand, and she got a little more grace from others because people chalked it up to being young and to traditional stand-by-your-man patriarchy by staying with her husband through his sentence. His short sentence also meant that he was labeled as more "redeemable" since he would be out relatively quickly, meaning he was in for something less offensive or less stigmatized. A long sentence comes with harsh judgment: "Why would you get twenty years if you didn't do something terrible?" And that judgment transfers: "Something must be wrong with you if you're staying with a person who goes to prison for a long time." We didn't find the support that we needed or were looking for from our blood family, but we found everything that we longed for in one another. Each of us had something to offer, whether it was monetary, a car, a place to lay our heads, the gift of gab, but most importantly we felt seen and heard by one another, and that's all we needed to create something so special: our family.

When my granny taught me to cook, it wasn't through recipes; she taught me to cook with my senses: vision, hearing, taste, touch, and smell. Making our community was a delicate balance; it was like making my ramen. Like the Maruchan package, the prison only came with two ingredients: follow the rules and always remember that visiting is "a privilege and not a right." Don't get me wrong, you could use just the basic ingredients like I did on my first visit to Calipatria, but it wouldn't be satisfying. If you wanted something that tasted good, that kept you warm and sustained you, you definitely had to add your own ingredients.

Community Spread

Serves 4–600 people
Preparation time: Weekdays
Cooking time: One weekend weekly

INGREDIENTS

A spot in line	Backups
A place to stay	Conversational skills
Proximity	Quick thinking
Cars (at least 2)	Distractors
Money	Trust

DIRECTIONS

The first step is to set your foundation and figure out how to get your place in line. This determines the time and quality of your visit. If you don't have a space in line, you're spending hours to travel for a few moments of visitation. If you want to enjoy your visit, feeling rested is crucial, so if you have your space in line taken care of, you can rest easy so long as you have a place to stay. Hotels, particularly those near a prison, are expensive and not great quality. So having a space that feels like home near the prison ensures you feel rested for your visit. If you can have an apartment or a place you can consistently call your own nearby it, this makes the entire visit more worthwhile. This is part of the proximity; you can stay somewhere nice, but that might compromise your space in line, which means your rest is for nothing. If you're not close to the prison, you're going to have to start over the next weekend and try to make a community spread from scratch.

The car is a two-step situation because you need two drivers: one who can come up early and leave their car to hold your spot in line, and one to pick up the other driver from the spot in line. If you have only one car, you can try to use a substitute, like traffic cones or something that looks official, to hold your space in line, but two cars and two people make everyone's day go smoother.

Money is the binder that holds the whole spread together. Of course you have to pay for the housing, the cars, the gas, the essentials to get you to and from a visit. But you need money for all the unexpected incidentals—maybe the person renting the apartment is short on funds one week, maybe gas prices go up, maybe life happens and there's just a need for more money. Everyone has to pitch in to make a community pot. This goes for backups too. Life always happens—people get sick, cars break down, mandatory

OT at work from the weekdays. You need backups lined up to fill some needs. Maybe somebody goes on vacation rather than a visit during the weekend. You have to be ready for the unexpected, and the spread will fill in the gaps that are left by people having lives.

Of course, what makes this work are the intangibles that you can bring to the table. Everyone has quirks and qualities that make the spread come together, but there are four intangibles that make the whole operation work. On the surface, you have to have the conversational skills—you need people who can talk to the state in any language the state understands. You have to make the COs think you're not a threat, that you're not "like the rest of them." And make them think you're friends. That opens everything up to let you get what you want. Maybe you're not the first in line every weekend, but if you know the COs, they make sure your loved one is the first one out the door to come to visitation. Maybe you're doing more hand-holding than the manual allows, or your kid wants multiple hugs and kisses with their parent; if you have talked up the COs, they can look the other way. This isn't an ordinary small-talk situation; it's an understanding that when you're coming to visit, no matter how friendly a guard might be and you might be to a guard, y'all are never friends. Maybe friend*ly*, but never friends. The guards are the ones who help to keep the prison working, and it's just a job, but at the end of the day their concern is for their job, not for us. And a lot of the time it's not even the job. It's about power—yes, the job does something that sustains you and pays well and supports your family. One thing about visiting prisons for decades is you notice changes in everything, but especially the people. I've seen people start with braces, fresh out of high school, working as guards. They may start nice and respectful or start out harsh because it's what they're told to do. But no matter how they start with the prison, it quickly becomes about the power they wield over other people. The rules take less of a purpose. They're not about safety or a regulation or a reason; the rules become a purpose in themselves. Another way of control and power over other people. The people inside the prison and the community that comes to visit them every weekend. Our concern is for our families, not their jobs or the little power trips they be on. Friend*ly*, but never friends.

It's a dynamic, a dance of conversation, but you need to supplement the conversational skills with quick thinking and distractions. To keep the conversation friendly, you have to be fast on your feet to talk to the guards. You get caught wearing a piece of clothing that's out of regulation, you have to watch the guards. If someone is watching you too long, they're about to say something about what you're wearing, so you have to read the situation to talk to them. To get their mind off the policies and onto the door, onto the person they see in front of them. If you think about people instead of policy, the conversation goes easier, and you can make the policy fit the person. You have to also think quickly to read everyone around you. Gang politics are a big part of prison, but when you're visiting you're all bunched and bundled into these rooms together, so you have to not fall into the same traps of being pitted against one another which sometimes happens to folks on the inside. So now you have to read the room and know what's going on around you to see if you have to talk your way out of a conflict between two people on the inside by talking on the outside. But quick thinking also means taking advantage and even creating distractions. You need someone who is sweet and unassuming to challenge the assumptions of the guards and the system. Someone who could never possibly do anything wrong, someone who draws attention from the guards in a nonconfrontational way that makes the guards take notice of what you want noticed—the friendliness of the group, the fact that one person might need a little more help—rather than what you don't want noticed, like a dress-code violation or contraband (because everything is contraband, even an extra dollar for the vending machine).

But the final ingredient, what makes the entire spread pop, is trust. When oppressed folks are trying to survive and organize in a place that is not meant for them to survive, trust is always a part of the equation. We have to be able to trust one another with our lives. The consequences of this type of orchestration can be grave. If there are any shenanigans and somebody gets caught, everybody gets caught, and a whole new chain reaction goes off. Some of the group might have a record or even warrants. A loss of visitation is always at stake, because "it's a privilege, not a right," but the consequences are harsh on the outside too. Maybe you wind up in prison on the mainline rather than visiting as a mainline mama.

REGULARS

By 2006 I had everything figured out. My system was down. The line figured out. Who to talk to? I knew all their names. Every *t* was crossed, every *i* was dotted. Visiting prison was as mindless as getting up to go to work. Just another routine. But then Jason told me he was getting transferred. I was about to lose everything again. I'd spent the past year visiting prison with Chastity, Dana, Michelle, Danielle, and Angela—even though Michelle faded away and stopped coming, especially after she and Chastity had a kinda quiet falling-out. Danielle's dude had short time, so she fizzled out faster than anyone. Angela's mother got sick, and she had to reshift her priorities again. Me, Chastity, and Dana were the last three regulars, but that trio was now going down to two. I was going to have to learn a new place.

At first it seemed like a regular phone call, just like we did every day. Jason had been trying to get a lower-level prison for years—he had been on level four for the past ten years, the whole time he had been locked up. California ranked all incarcerated people with a "placement score" and ranked prisons by the security level. Violent crime, weapons, gang enhancements, the type of felony—they up your placement score. The higher the placement score, the higher the security level. The higher the security level, the less rights inside, and the less privileges you get in visitation. Jason got sentenced for a carjacking (felony), attempted involuntary manslaughter (violent felony), and using a gun (weapon enhancement)—he got lucky they didn't prove the gang enhancement, but he was already going to level four, so that would have only changed his sentence, not his placement. Every year you might get points taken away for good behavior or points added for anything they classified as bad behavior. A nice little Ponzi scheme. Jason had went to reclassification every year for the past ten years, trying to show that he wasn't getting write-ups, that he was going to school, learning a trade. It sounds simple, but a write-up can be for any violation of the rules—anything from listening too slow when they ask you to get up, to a full-on melee. It takes a long time for points to come off, and there's no guarantee; the committee has to approve everything. Even with visitation, the privilege is not a right, and that only comes with full-time work and keeping in compliance. So you have to work to get points off, work to keep getting visited, work to get your two cents an hour added to your canteen that you only get full access to if you work, work to get more than one phone call a week, work to get a package. Prison labor isn't just the people you might see in the movies working a chain gang or cleaning up the side of the highway, wearing bright orange with a cop with a shotgun on a horse. Prison is six full-time jobs.

So when Jason was finally reclassified as a level three, I didn't think that it would change the prison or the routine. I figured it would mean some more privileges and less bullshit for him as he finished the second half of his sentence. It was a shock to me that we were about to move. After his two years at Calipatria, I was ready for that to be the routine for the rest of his twenty years. Sure, he had been moved before, from High Desert to Calipatria, but that had been closer. So I was hopeful. Jason heard he was going to Ironwood, but he didn't know anything about the place, just what he heard from other dudes on the inside. When I got the time to look it up for myself, it eased some of my anxiety. Ironwood is in Blythe, California, maybe two hours away from Calipatria, but ironically it didn't really change up my drive—for Calipat you get off the 10 and take the 111, but for Blythe you just stay on the 10 until you're there. But this move wasn't like with High Desert, because now I knew that things change from prison to prison. I knew each prison has its own system, and I had no idea what system I was about to get into. Each prison has their own structure of how the line works and how life works on the outside. Some prisons won't even allow you near the property until visitation time starts. Now that I knew what life was like at the front of the line, I wasn't going back to the back. I had to finish up the call with Jason like normal, but there was no sense in talking to him about all this. He wasn't having to relearn the system.

But as soon as we hung up, I was calling Chastity. She had more points of reference from visiting multiple prisons. This wasn't her first rodeo. Chasity is compassionate, but her mouth is reckless: "Damn. That's fucked up. They're trying to take away my friend." Even good news has bad news. We got out all our "Damn," "That's fucked up," "This is stupid"s for a few minutes before Chastity went into problem-solving mode. "Ay, no, this will be fine. I've been to Ironwood before. It's been a minute, but the line works pretty much the same way." She got right to the perks of being at Ironwood: "Girl, you're gonna be good. There the line might be a little easier because it's a level three, so it ain't gonna be busy as fuck like these Calipat visits. You're about to get family visits frequent as fuck because there's not a lotta people there that are on level three. Two, you aren't going to have to deal with these Calipat bitches." Calipatria was ridiculously crowded. If you commit a supermax crime in LA, you wind up in Pelican Bay, somewhere far away. But if your points are lower, you wind up at Calipat, as a level four. Nobody is going up to High Desert, Folsom, Pelican Bay, on a regular basis. But once you get down to Calipat, or Donovan by San Diego, that means it's drivable. But if it's easier for you, it's easier for everyone else. That means everyone from different hoods going out to visit at the same prisons. That means crowds and conflicts that you now have to navigate. And Chastity, of course, saw the bright side. "Oh, now you're about to be on family visits once a month." Now that Jason and I were married, we got rights to family visit. At Calipatria this was maybe once every ninety days. The policy was so spaced out because so many people were at the prison that everybody was trying to get a family visit as often as they could. But with me out at Ironwood, now there would be less people, and a little more of a drive meant less regular visitors and more time for me and my family.

Now, a family visit is the best you can hope for when your loved one is locked up. The "conjugal visit" has a lot of mythology around it and gets thrown around in different ways in different states and places. Some states, like Mississippi, where my cousin Antwoine was locked up for ten years, had their conjugal visits strictly limited to a person you were married to, in a room adjacent to the main visiting room, private, but during regular visiting hours. Not my idea of an intimate time, so I'm glad I never had to figure that out. In California a family visit meant that you not only got normal visiting hours; you got some options. You could go on a Wednesday and leave Friday, or go on a Friday and leave Sunday. When you're living and seeing your loved one for maybe six hours a week (seven hours on paper, but that eight a.m. to three p.m. schedule doesn't count the time you spend getting in and out of the prison, so it's really six hours if you're lucky, attentive, and know how to work the system) every moment matters. So a family visit isn't just extra time; it's everything.

With a family visit you get privacy. You aren't in the visitation room; you have a little space to yourselves. At Calipatria they had little houses they built on the property—manufactured stucco homes that blended into the desert. Nothing fancy, just a stand-alone house, with a square shape and flat roof, a desert-grass lawn that went brown in the summertime, surrounded by a fence—a high, maybe forty-foot-tall, chain-link fence at the top. The little cement walkway led from the fenced entrance to the door of the home. Inside was a tiled floor everywhere—the cheap off-white vinyl that lines every school cafeteria because it comes in bulk and is easy to clean. Inside the door is a nice living-room space with a chocolate brown couch, the type you might get for next to nothing from a thrift store when you first move out on your own. Surprisingly comfortable for what it was, more comfort than you would ever expect from a prison. A little wooden TV stand with an old-school tubed-box TV sitting on the stand. Something too heavy for anybody to pick up, move, or do anything with. The kitchen had one seventies table—a small circle made entirely of wood, free-standing, surrounded by four chairs made of metal but padded with that floral faux-leather plastic that looked like they had been there forever. The kitchen had a very generic little white-box fridge, with a generic stove, sink, and microwave. Nothing was bolted down, so the family visit really pretended like the prison trusted some people. A surprising amount of freedom, if you didn't look out the windows and see the high fence, barbed wire, and armed guards walking around. It was easy to forget where you were if you closed all the doors and drew the curtains. You even had a bathroom, with a full sink, toilet, tub, and shower. A bathtub was huge for Jason, because he had been sharing showers for the past decade, and you don't get to sit in water. A family-visit house is luxury for people on the inside, all the small luxuries you take for granted. And that's before even we get to the comfort of the bedroom. A queen-size mattress on a box spring—no headboard or anything fancy. Two generic nightstands next to the bed, with a light on the ceiling and a corded phone installed to the wall. This wasn't a phone for the outside; this was a phone to the guards, for them to check in. Little freedoms still came with control and surveillance, and over the weekend the guard could call on the phone to check in and make sure Jason was still there. Quaint suburban family, but make it prison.

A family visit meant space to ourselves—still under the eye of the state, but with a taste of privacy outside the immediate gaze of the COs and other visitors. The state was watching, but you didn't feel as watched, didn't have the need to be as performative as possible. You had to be dress-code compliant when you checked in and came to the prison, but inside your little family-visit house you could wear and act and move how you wanted. You weren't constantly being reminded of where you were, what the limits were, and somebody threatening to jump in on your space. The same rules applied for entering the prison for visitation—general visit or family visit—but inside the family visit you had your own space between yourselves as a family.

The kitchen was my favorite luxury, because now we could cook. What set Calipatria and Ironwood apart was the kitchens. In Calipatria, the prison mailed me a list of ingredients I could buy in advance. Full groceries. Three pounds of ground beef. A dozen eggs. Spaghetti noodles. Sauce. Seasonings. I could make my spaghetti. Cook actual chicken. I didn't want to spend a whole weekend eating gas-station burgers and frozen burritos. To create some semblance of my normal meant a lot, but for Jason, to bring that sense of home right to him was special. Everything inside the prison, even in the cafeteria, was powdered and boxed and made for mass consumption. That meant bland. That meant shelf-stable and something that could be served in quantities to scale. Inside our family-visit room I could make a meal just for us. I could season and flavor in the ways I wanted to, rather than just with whatever was in the little seasoning packet. I once ordered salad to make as a side, and Jason told me he hadn't had lettuce since before he got locked up.

More family visits were the biggest perk I could imagine, and Chastity knew that would calm me down. But I knew inside that meant I was losing my spot in the line at Calipatria. I would have to figure out a new space, with new people, and a new system—even if it was similar to the one at Calipatria, I'd have to start over.

Moving prisons isn't a to-do or transition. I found out from Jason on a weekday that he was moving prisons, so that meant my whole routine got interrupted because he got moved. Now I had to tell Dana and Chastity I was all the way done with our routine, and I had to start anew. No goodbyes, no farewell tour, just an end, and a new start at a new place.

But we knew what it was. We might not see one another every weekend, but we could still see one another. We had transcended this weekend prison shit; we were family. We were locked in, not locked up. I could still invite Chastity and Dana to all the things. If I had a family visit, I could still drop my car off with Chastity at Calipatria; she'd drive me up to Ironwood for the weekend and use my car while I was inside with Jason. It was the end of my visits at Calipatria, but with all this experience under my belt, I was not scared or anxious. I was a regular, and I knew what I was doing. I was a full-fledged mainline mama.

We started calling ourselves the regulars as a way of showing we were about that life. The COs, other people around the town and at the prison, started to know us as "regulars" because we would come every weekend. We knew the ins and the outs. We were knowing, and more importantly, we were *known*. People might not have known us, but they knew who we were. But being a regular isn't a label you apply to yourself or you talk about on your own time. A regular is something you get called once you start visiting enough that the COs who work there know your face, and so they start identifying you as a regular who visits. Regulars are everyone who visits the prison often enough to become known to the space of the prison. We were regulars, but so were the church-lady moms who visited their children on the weekend. The missionaries who came every weekend to convert people on the inside to whatever faith or denomination they represented were regulars too. Women who were just starting a relationship with somebody on the inside on some pen-pal situation and came to visit for a few weekends at a time were regulars too. Sometimes you had folks who had a marriage on the inside but had their own situations on the outside. In normal life we might have thought of it as a form of polyamory—there was serious and intimate commitment between the spouses, and the incarcerated partner knew what it was, but the partner on the outside was living their own life, going on dates, having sex and whole other relationships with the full knowledge of their spouse on the inside, but the commitment never stopped. These women were regulars too. Regulars came in every type of person, every shape and size, but what drew us all together was coming to the prison every weekend, or every other weekend, or often enough to become known around the prison by the guards and the other visitors. Not all women visiting a prison were regulars, but all the regulars were for sure women. Maybe you saw a dad, a cousin, or an uncle come visit for the holidays or a special occasion, but that was it. The regulars were women committed to somebody on the inside, and who committed to the process of visiting.

But even among the regulars there's a special category of us who don't just come to visit for our family and don't just visit for the sake of visiting. Sometimes you visit for yourself or for your loved one on the inside. And sometimes you visit just to stick it to the state that thinks that incarceration is a good thing to do to people. The state that thinks it can keep people apart and break them down. Regular visits exploit people on the inside and outside—because "visitation is a privilege and not a right." It's encouragement for good behavior for people locked up, and a way to control people on the outside who want to see their family. When you're a regular who visits for family and you navigate the process of visitation and family on the inside and outside, you engage in a type of mothering that puts you in a position to care for everybody around you in the most radical act of love that is diametrically opposed to what a prison is constructed to do. This is the mainline mama.

Prison is the face of rehabilitation, to put adults in a time-out for bad behavior, but that sentence is on the person incarcerated and everyone they belong to in their community. A mainline mama is a fuck-you to incarceration. Being a regular means caring for and coming to see the person on the inside. Being a mainline mama turns the visitation and process that the prison wants into a lifestyle that is meaningful and fulfilling. We take what the state gives us and make it our own. We take the ingredients and turn it into a spread, in our own way, on our own time. The joy we found in the space in the prison wasn't just in our romantic attachments. It was not a love between me and Jason that was bringing me the full joy of life that gave me meaning in those weekend visits. I found community and love with Chastity and Dana, and Michelle, Danielle, and Angela when they were there. We cared for one another, we cared for our people on the inside, we cared for our family on the outside. And the state exploited our care because "visitation is a privilege and not a right," and used our mothering and radical love and care against us to try and control our people on the inside. But we loved and cared and showed up regularly anyway, because the state can try and use our love for its own purposes, but it doesn't own our love or the way we show it. We are in control, no matter how the state tries to flex and show it is in charge—and might actually be, with the fences and guards and guns that keep people doing what the state wants. But the acts of care and mothering and compassion that a mainline mama shows are pure love that is a radical defiance of the state. I became a regular in the first few weeks at Calipatria, but by the second month I was a mainline mama. I knew how to make our visits at Calipatria seamless in a couple of weeks. By the end of the second month I knew it was love between us at Chastity's little apartment. How else could I explain *actually enjoying* spending my adult weekends sleeping in a one-bedroom apartment with three other grown women?

● ● ●

My first visit to Ironwood was different than any first visit I ever had—the first visit at county jail, at High Desert, at Calipatria, all had me anxious and scared for different reasons. At county jail, I was still a *minor*, there to visit someone I was in a relationship with. I had to take my granny with me to visit Jason, who had just turned eighteen, so I had to manufacture reasons to visit to make sure Jason wasn't getting put on the radar for anything that would put him in more trouble. Plus, he was a light-skinned—white-passing—Mexican man, and I was very clearly a dark-skinned Black girl, so there was no that's-my-cousin faking to make it easy. At High Desert, it was far as fuck away, a supermax prison, when Jason and I weren't even on the best terms. The weird, uneasy feeling every visit because we were mentally and emotionally in different spaces that were far from our comfort zone, physically and emotionally. And if we weren't on the same page mentally during the visit, I was mad because I just wasted fourteen hours for Jason to get on my nerves, and he was mad because he waited and built up this whole visit for it to be me being mad. At Calipatria I was excited about the proximity of it all, but once I saw it go from three cars to three hundred, I knew I was in over my head until I found my people and became a real mainline mama.

Now at Ironwood, for the first time I was coming in with an awareness and a purpose. Just because I was new to this prison didn't mean I was new to this game. I was a mainline mama. I was not new to this; I was true to this. I drove the same drive from my house in Hesperia, taking the I-10 out of LA, through Chino, through Palm Springs, through the desert, all the way to the borderlands at Blythe, right on the edge of California and Arizona. This was my first visit, so I was coming in early to scope the whole sitch-ee-ation. If there was a line, I was preparing for it. I left work Friday—my kids were big enough to stay home on their own at this point, so they were set—and I got to Blythe right around midnight and pulled up to Ironwood to see the scene. I saw cars already parked on the road up to the prison, so I knew there were at least other regulars here. Maybe ten cars were already in line, but now I knew what was what. A couple of the cars had people in them to stay for the night, but most of them were empty, so I knew there were people here who knew the system, and the system here was like the one at Calipatria. I went to park my car at the back of the line, but it was midnight, and I didn't know nobody here, and I didn't want to go find a hotel and spend money, and the people here didn't know me. Midnight was close enough to the time that I could sleep in my car, brush my teeth, wash my face, and be ready for a visit in the morning. I came prepared. I drove after I had taken a shower and washed as best I could and got in my jammies, and I had brought my real clothes for the visit. Luckily, I had my laptop, with its little DVD drive. So I climbed in the back seat with my blanket and my covers. I popped in my DVDs to watch movies until I fell asleep in the back of my little Honda Accord at the back of the line.

I jolted up from my alarm clock. The desert at night was cold as fuck, so I was huddled up with not enough blankets. I had to pee so bad. But I needed to know how big this line was. This was my first time, and I had to scope out the scene. If I was by myself at this prison, I didn't want to have to come around midnight every time. I looked back out the rear window; there were cars, but I couldn't tell how many. So I looked out front for any of the cars in front to see who might have a grip on the system. Nobody in front had arrived yet, so I stepped out of the car to get a better view of the line behind me. Long as fuck, just like at Calipat. Time to start my routine in the car.

I climbed back into the driver's seat and started my routine. I had a water bottle set aside just for flossing and brushing my teeth. After my teeth were taken care of, I used a pack of baby wipes to wash my face and started putting on my lotion. I changed out of my long nightshirt and leggings into my visiting clothes. Very regular, very dress-code appropriate. And now time to sit and wait.

Unlike Calipatria, Ironwood would not let anyone onto the prison grounds until 7:45. Ironwood is easy to get to from LA because you stay on the 10, get off the exit, and take the long desert road to the front of the prison. Nothing but tumbleweeds to keep you company. Ironwood really has two prisons right next to each other on the same property, so the winding road leading up is a public road that you can park on. But once you get to the edge of the prison, there's a guard shack and a giant sign warning you that the public road ends at the guard shack and not to enter the prison grounds. So when you're in line, there's nothing to do but wait in line until the guard drives up from the prison to give the cars the okay.

My laptop was deader than dead at this point, so I was waiting for the guards and other cars, just sitting in my car, listening to music. Around 7:15 I saw a car pull up toward the front of the line, so I sat up straight so I could take notice. I couldn't see the people or their faces, but I noticed the car. I can't even remember what type of car it was, but that morning I had it memorized because I could tell they had a system, and their system looked like what me, Chastity, Michelle, and Dana had at Calipatria. I kept taking mental notes so I could bide my time and approach them when it was right. Nobody was looking to have conversations right now; everybody was waiting for the guard. The line is no place to be chopping it up with a stranger; you got to be ready to go. If you're sitting around, not paying attention when that guard says it's time to come in, people are going around you. And nobody lines up and waits that long just to get passed up.

Once the guard comes out and waves the cars in, it turns all our cars into preschoolers. One at a time. Single-file line. Slow and easy. But every car has to stop at the actual gate to the prison. Each car gets stopped at the gate for inspection. You have to present your ID—valid photo ID only, nothing expired or your visit is getting canceled. Then you get your pass with a number on it, and you wait as the guard inspects the car—looks in the windows, pops the trunk. Once you pass the gate, it's into the prison visitors' parking lot. It's a parking lot. Cement and desert.

I got out of my car and spotted the car that I saw at the front of the line earlier that morning. I was watching and sizing them up to figure out who would be easiest to approach. One of the women was Black, with deep dark skin like my cousin Antwoine, but short and heavyset with flowy hair down to the middle of her back. One of the women looked like so many of the Mexican girls I went to junior high with in LA; she had wings painted by her eyes, skinny little chola eyebrows, hair half-up and half-down. She had a baby with her in a little car-seat carrier. One was solid, a good six feet, and built, with long, flowing wavy hair, but I couldn't place her, maybe Pacific Islander or mixed. Everyone was getting out of their cars and walking up to the visitor processing center. Even though they let you on the grounds around 7:45, they would not let you into the visiting center until eight. No earlier. Luckily, there were bleachers and chairs set up near the entrance, so you could rest while you waited. But they didn't care if it was rainy or there was wind blowing or any kind of weather; they would sit inside and watch you until it was eight on the dot. Everyone had their numbers already when you passed through the gate, so there was no new line, just people waiting around for eight to roll around so the doors would open.

This was my window to talk to the women I saw at the front of the line. I walked right up to the Black woman in the group, because we Black and it's just that simple. "Hey, can I talk to you for a minute? My name's Keeonna. What's your name?" She said, "Mo'nique." I gave her my little pitch: "This is my first time at Ironwood. I used to go to Calipat. I see you got your car at the front; do you come every weekend? If so, can we exchange information, and can I roll with y'all?" I had to drop the keywords to make it clear: this was my first time here, but this was not my first rodeo. I could tell that they might have been regulars, but I had to make sure. Mo'nique was very friendly. "Oh, okay. Yeah, I come with Raye and Melissa," she said, pointing to the tall woman and the Mexican woman I saw her riding in the car with. I found out they got the same situation we had at Calipatria. Raye lived in town, and Mo'nique would come up on Fridays. I'd come to find out she changed her work schedule so she didn't have to work on Fridays so she could come up. They had the same shit crackin' we had at Calipatria. I couldn't believe it. I didn't think we had invented something new, but what we had at Calipatria felt special and creative, like Chastity had really figured out the whole system. But smart ideas can pop up anywhere, and people were really sleeping in their cars every week like I had last night. So it made sense that other women would figure out the system to make this whole weekend life work.

Mo'nique introduced me to Raye and Melissa and welcomed me in. Mo'nique and I exchanged numbers even though it wasn't her house or her car, but Mo'nique was the boss of the situation. I'd find out later that Raye was between jobs at the time—her dude on the inside she had actually met while she was working a job at the prison, so when they got together for real she had to quit—and so Mo'nique was helping her out by making all the other regulars who stayed at her place give her some money to hold her over during the week and so she could spend on the weekends. Mo'nique was the total package: the boss, the brains, and the muscle. She concocted the whole situation and made sure that everybody was taken care of in the group.

My experience at Calipatria gave me enough experience to make everything here happen seamlessly. Everything about the routine at Ironwood was the same situation—taking turns to leave the car, staying the night at the apartment in town—only now I was giving Raye a little bit of money to stay at her house for the weekend. But that little thirty-five dollars was a small entry fee to stay at somebody's house for two nights, especially considering the hotel options in the town. I had got used to paying no money at Chastity's house in Calipatria, but this was better than paying the seventy-five dollars a night at the Motel 6 down the street. I don't trust a Motel 6, so I was not about to pay a hundred fifty dollars a weekend to stay at some bullshit-ass motel when I could give Raye thirty-five dollars and know what I was getting into. Plus, I got a spot in the line, and that let me sleep in more and have people to enjoy my time with.

Blythe is a prison town, and they have the game rigged. It's in the middle of the desert; it's a stop through a town that people might come by if they are on their way to California or Arizona. But on the weekends everybody in town knew there were people like me who were coming in to visit at the prison. And all the prices at the motels got mysteriously higher on the weekends. The Motel 6, Super 8, and the raggedy little local motel cost way more than they were worth because they knew they could get it. These local motels weren't super well kept, but they were the only game in town. The few times I had to stay in a Blythe motel, there was always some bullshit with the prices, or it wasn't well kept, or just something went wrong that made the whole weekend rougher.

So being able to stay with Raye and ride with her, Mo'nique, and Melissa not only saved me money but this was me setting up my friendships and relationships all by myself. Unlike with Chastity, where Anthony and Jason helped set it up from the inside, providing their own vetting and sign-offs, this was all me and Mo'nique. No men involved, just mainline mamas. It was better they weren't involved too, because Jason and Mo'nique's husband, Brooklyn, were on completely different yards, so if they even wanted to talk, it would be sending a kite to talk to the other yard, passing notes through a bunch of other people. That's all waiting. But then Jason and Brooklyn were also in different gangs. Brooklyn was a Crip, but he wasn't trippin' on Jason. Jason was Blood-affiliated but supposedly inactive and sitting back as an OG, but just on principle Jason was upset that Brooklyn was a Crip. Not that Jason heard anything or that he knew Brooklyn from anywhere in or outside the prison—just on the principle, like Jason was fifteen years old and had just jumped in, trying to show

how serious he was. But I didn't care. This was between me and Mo'nique, and Mo'nique seemed cool as hell.

Sometimes friendships take a while to develop as you get to know each other, but like some people fall in love at first sight; me and Mo'nique were super close friends from that day forward. "Oh, you from LA? I'm from LA!" She was Crip-affiliated; I was from a Crip neighborhood. And then we started driving together too. We started taking turns driving. We would meet in Moreno Valley, and park our cars in a residential area by a KFC, and pick whose car we were driving out to Blythe, and just go. We started close and got even closer over the drives and getting to know each other. From Moreno Valley to Blythe is two and a half hours on a good day, so that was just a long conversation. Relationships and family were all on the table; we could chop it up the whole ride.

But I got to *know* know Mo'nique through her music. I could always tell her mood by her music. She was always making mixtapes and playlists or bringing her CDs on the drive. If she was playing Ginuwine's "I'm in Love" or Plies's "Shawty" with T-Pain, it was gonna be a good visit for her. If she was on some Chris Brown's "Ya Man Ain't Me," she was letting everyone know "I'm thicker than a Snicker, but I can get anybody I want," because Brooklyn was on some bullshit with some bad phone calls or arguments. She would still go visit, and she was always nice to me, but the music would tell me if it was going to be a lovey visit or if she was just going to cuss Brooklyn's ass out in person. Mo'nique was body positivity before Lizzo made it a thing. Especially in that time around 2008: if you were even a couple pounds overweight, people would automatically brand you as ugly, and when you're visiting a prison, people assume you're being used. It's a way of saying that nobody would want you because you're big, so the only reason you must be visiting prison is because you're being used. Brooklyn was thin and nice-looking too, with that swag and bravado about him that made him attractive. So when people say a mainline mama is being "used" just because other people think her looks don't match her man on the inside, that's the worst thing you can say. Being "used" is a dig because it makes you so ugly that the only way you can be found lovable is with someone who has no other choice. It removes all agency from a woman, underestimating how women can pull in dudes no matter their looks or shape. And for Mo'nique and Brooklyn, they had been together since they were kids, and married long before he got locked up. When Mo'nique was feeling it with Brooklyn, she was in love. She was singing her songs in the car and just talking about how much more she loved Brooklyn than I loved Jason. "And you know why? Because every kiss begins with *K*," she would sing. She didn't care that my name started with *K* and she couldn't win, but you could feel the love between Mo'nique and Brooklyn with your whole heart.

● ● ●

Mo'nique and I got along from day one, and she brought me into her little group with Raye and Michelle, but not everybody who visited the prison was built like us. Together we were living the life as mainline mamas. We took care of one another and leaned on one another. We mothered one another, and when I would bring my kids, Mo'nique would take care of them. Mo'nique was always buying shit for Michelle's baby, who Mo'nique named "Fatty," and would take that baby with her to her visits with BK. If Mo'nique didn't have the money for a rental to drive out to Blythe for the weekend, instead of meeting in Moreno Valley I'd drive to LA and pick her up. Even though we were all giving Raye money to stay at her place, nothing was transactional. That was just taking care of one another. But not everybody who visited every weekend was a mainline mama like us; some were just regulars. We would see regulars every weekend because we all went to the same place and we were friendly, but nobody was talking deeply or being about each other's business. Just other faces you saw regularly.

But not everybody who visits prison is a regular. Sometimes you had a visit from the weekend warriors—people who come every so often but loved to start shit. These are the people who try to pull up to the front of the line at the guard post at 7:20 a.m. and act like they didn't see the sea of cars sitting behind them, waiting to go in. Then if you call them out or if anybody says anything, they're either gonna play stupid—"Well, I didn't see anyone, I don't know"—like they didn't see the line, or be mad at us for being at the front of the line. The weekend warriors aren't regulars, but they come regularly, maybe four times a year. And then when they try to skip the line, they want to make it an issue with us mainline mamas. "Why do you get to be at the front of the line?" or "You left your car here, that's not fair." It wasn't our fault we figured out the game and played it like experts every weekend.

Even worse than the weekend warriors were the charter bus people. Every few months there would be some charter bus company based out of LA that would bring folks from LA to Blythe, but people on the bus would treat it like their forty-dollar bus fare bought them VIP tickets to the show. The charter bus would pull up at seven thirty at the very front of the line. It passed all the cars and figured because it was a big bus, it could jump everybody who had waited and waited every weekend in the same way. But the bus thought it knew what was best, and it always started a fight. The disrespect for the mainline mamas, regulars, and even weekend warriors who spent their whole weekend—and most of us every weekend—staying in town, staying in line, maybe living out of a car, and making all kinds of sacrifices to be there. Now a whole charter bus full of people thought it could pull to the front of the line and take somebody from number ten to number eighty just because it was a bus.

You waited all that time to get cut ahead in line, and now everybody was mad. People on the bus were mad because they felt entitled—they paid their forty dollars, and they wanted door-to-door service. People in the line were mad because they knew what was going on, and everything the bus was doing broke all the rules. But nobody wanted to mess their visit up because everybody had waited all this time. So all these tensions and anger were bubbling at the start of the day, and the COs didn't want to get involved because that was a big group of people to deal with. The biggest consequence they can give is canceling people's visits for the day. So nobody wants to start a fight, at least not right then and there. The only times there were fights at visitation was when that bus came, and when two women showed up to visit the same dude. But no matter the reason for the fight, people are not willing to sacrifice visitation time over some bullshit. That's why you wait. So if visitation ends at 2:45, people are going to leave a little early so you can be waiting in the parking lot and make sure that you can holler at whoever had a problem earlier that day. Then the fight happens; beefs are settled in the parking lot with a fight until somebody gives up, gets tired, or one of the friends breaks it up. But always after visitation, because nobody is giving up their time.

And the fights have to happen because that is another violation of the code of mainline mamas and regulars. Everybody is there on an honor system, built on mutual respect. You look and listen, try to understand the situation before you start telling everybody else what to do. Because no matter what prison you go to, there's going to be somebody who's been visiting there before you; there's already a system and a code and a routine. Newcomers don't get to question or turn the whole system upside down just because they're new.

Mainline mamas work on trust and an honor system that we all rely on. And sometimes that goes sideways. We're all mainline mamas, and when somebody tries to position themselves as the center of the universe, it turns things wrong. There's no one person above the group. So when people start acting like it's David Ruffin and the Temptations rather than just The Temptations, things go sideways. When you have a system that's built on trust, if people start breaking rules that you've all set together and are playing in your face, there's no coming back from a breach of trust. Mainline mamas take care of one another and our kids, so when people stop caring for one another, they stop being mainline mamas and just be regulars.

● ● ●

Me and Mo'nique were close from day one, and we celebrated our friendship and celebrated each other. Mo'nique, Melissa, and Raye all fell out a few months into my visits to Ironwood, so we didn't get a chance for all four of us to become close like me, Chastity, Dana, and Michelle. But with me and Mo'nique, we grew as friends and got to know some of the other cliques of mainline mamas that were coming through the prison. We weren't saving spaces for one another on the weekends, but we knew one another in the town, and we would enjoy one another's company after the visits.

It was important for all of us to make time for celebrations together. Being gone on the weekends to visit meant coming out to be with the person you loved at the prison, but it also meant you were missing out on life at home. The weekend birthday celebrations for friends, or just going out with my friends and family who I lived with on the weekdays. By this time I had a good job, and I was making good money. When I was at home and going out to dinner, we were talking Crustacean or Benihana, something nice. Mo'nique had a good job and made good money on the weekdays too, so most weekends we would treat ourselves after visitation and go to the nicest restaurant in Blythe: Sizzler. It was miles ahead of that vending-machine food we both hated in the prison, and it was still better than McDonald's. When they finally built a Popeyes and a Starbucks in Blythe, we thought we made it. But Sizzler became our home for celebrations. Weekends to make us feel special. Birthdays. Sizzler became the spot.

When the big holidays came up, me and Mo'nique would link up with some of the other cliques of mainline mamas we knew and would have a barbeque at the Motel 6 pool. Adults could have drinks; kids could hop in the pool. The motel had a little grill, but nobody was serious about grilling, and nobody was going to prepare food in their Motel 6 room. So instead, we would order a pile of pizzas from Domino's, and maybe some Popeyes once that got built. Everybody could lie out in the pool and have a good time. Mo'nique loved to swim and spent most of the time bragging about how she used to be a lifeguard at Lenny Krayzelburg Swim Academy.

All these little dinners and celebrations brought us closer and closer. It starts out with becoming friends with the women you see at the prison regularly on the weekends. Then you start to kick it after visitation hours, at dinner, spending your downtime together on the weekends before you head back to regular life. Then you start talking on the weekdays, checking up on each other, talking about the weekend and what's to come. With me and Mo'nique, we got even closer because she lived in LA, so we could kick it on the weekdays after work when we wanted to. That's how you go from being friends stuck in a situation to really becoming family. Now I had family at home in LA, and I had my family in Blythe—my husband, Jason, and my mainline mama family.

Mainline mamas become family because we build our relationships on trust and care, and we are the only ones who can understand the full experience. Becoming a mainline mama means dealing with the state and forging your own family connections beyond your blood family. Because even your blood family doesn't always understand why you do what you do—getting in line, sometimes staying in a car, driving for hours, dealing with the state, just to see the people you love. We're outsiders at the prison, outsiders in our own family. But not outsiders with one another. Family and friends at home look at you strange and don't get it. Even when family and friends at home try to be supportive, they're shaking their heads: "Better you than me," "If you like it, I love it," "Well, if it makes you happy." But they don't understand and don't try to. Mainline mamas don't have to try; we understand because we know. Mo'nique and Chastity gave me what my family and friends couldn't. Presence and absence. They were with me when I was at the prison on the weekend, and we talked and connected on the weekdays, when we weren't together. They didn't give me negative questions—no assumptions, no judgments. No prying to figure out life decisions. No shady caveats and qualifiers. The absence of negativity was something too few of my friends could figure out how to give me. I was, and still am, tired of being asked to overexplain my life and decisions. Everyone lives complex, multifaceted lives, but when you live as a mainline mama, that complexity goes out the window when friends and family who don't get it want to make everything about your choices. Yes, I chose to marry Jason; yes, I chose to keep my family together. But these were also the choices that I was told to make by my mom, my granny, society: *Marry the father of your children and be a real family.* What they didn't like were the consequences of what that meant. Being a family meant I was also living as a mainline mama, driving to the prison every week. It was hard for people to understand that, even people I thought I was so close to in every other way of life.

Ariana was one of my closest friends at work and after work. We hit the happy hours, went to Dave & Buster's for drinks, and hung out at her house. If I wasn't at the prison on a weekend— because if it was on lockdown from fights, visitation rights for the whole prison got lost, sometimes for weeks at a time—then I'd be at Ariana's house. One year it had been almost a month without visits because the prison was on lockdown week after week. Every week you had to call to see if visitation was available, and it had been weeks without it. For the first time in a long while, I spent time on the weekends with my home friends and family. I started going to regular events like a regular person, and Ariana invited me to her daughter's sixth birthday party, to hang out with my kids and her kids on the weekend.

The week of the party, I called the prison visitation line just to check, like I had every week for almost a month beforehand. "All yards are having visits this weekend." It was the message I was waiting to hear; I hadn't seen or heard from Jason for weeks. Lockdown means locked down. Maybe you can finesse somebody for a phone call real quick, but there's no contact. So when I heard the automated message, I was ready to go right then; I was beyond happy because I would finally get to see my family. When I hung up the phone, I saw Mo'nique had already texted me, "Bitch. It's visiting." Now I had to get ready for a weekend on short notice. But I also had to tell Ariana I wasn't going to make her daughter's party. She knew how long it had been since I got to see Jason, and by now Tre was thirteen and Eamon was eleven. Tre was too old and too teenage boy to enjoy a six-year-old girl's birthday party, and Eamon was staying with his dad every weekend by that point. So I didn't think it would be a big deal.

I called Ariana to tell her the good news and the bad news—I would get to see Jason, but I was going to miss her daughter's birthday party. She gave me a very generic "Aww, that's too bad." I tried to make it up to her and told her that if I wasn't tired after the visit, I would try to drive straight back so I could make it in the evening. "Oh, okay cool." I missed out on her daughter's birthday party, but I got to be with my family and see Jason for the first time in a month. Even though Mo'nique was going to visit too, I drove up by myself because Mo'nique got up early on Friday because she didn't have to work, and I still had to drive up Friday evening. But on Saturday, by the end of the visit, I was exhausted by the whirlwind of a last-minute visit, tired after the late-night drive on Friday. I didn't want to risk an accident rushing home on Saturday night, driving while sleepy, so immediately after visitation on Saturday afternoon, I called and told Ariana I wasn't going to make it back. "Oh, that's okay!"

I didn't even realize something was wrong until a couple days of Ariana not picking up my calls. Saturday night I tried to call just to see how the party went, no response. Sunday, no response. We talked every day, so now I was worried. Was there something wrong? Maybe something happened with her or her kid. No calls, no texts, nothing. A few days later she finally picked up my call, and she told me I had hurt her feelings by not coming to the party. I apologized because I really had meant to make it to the party, but I just hadn't expected there to be visitation. I kept falling over myself to explain the situation. In her eyes I had chosen to go visit a prison, chosen not to show up at her kid's birthday party. But I was hurt that my friend couldn't understand how important it was to go see my husband when we'd been cut off for weeks at a time. She lived with her husband. Got to see him every day. I didn't want my friend to be mad at me for just trying to enjoy what she got easy.

With other mainline mamas, there's no explanation. No shame, no searching for an answer that will appease. This is why our relationships are so important to us. Like, say I did stay home for Ariana's daughter's birthday or even my birthday weekend, and I went out with my friends and family at home. I would have an enjoyable time, but I wouldn't be fully present. Part of me would be there having fun, and the other part of me would be sad about missing my visit. This was the one time of the week I got to see Jason, and now it would be a whole week at best until the next time. And that was my life. And people didn't get it. People think mainline mamas are a weirdo spectacle, and even when we're home we don't fit in because it's fucking weird to the family. It's weird.

The real world is allowed to move on without you, but you're not allowed to move on without it. Every weekend I would visit the prison, my friends and family had no problem moving right along with their lives. They weren't rearranging dates to the week-days to make it work around my family schedule, and I didn't hold that against them. Life went on, I missed out, and I made my choice to be with my family that I didn't get to be with every day. For everybody else you might not see your family every day, but you have that option. The possibility is still there. My only chance to see my husband was a *maybe* six-hour window on a Saturday when the prison wasn't locked down. I chose to go to the prison because I had no other choice about when I got to see my family. If I could choose for Jason to be available more, I would. But being a mainline mama means family puts a weird emphasis on the choice of going to a prison. Any relationship should be rooted in choice, but choosing to go to a prison is a decision that comes without empathy. There's little recognition of how limited time there is to visit, of how you don't get to see each other, other than those few hours on the weekend. Oh well, you signed up for it. The consequences of my choice were treated like a punishment I inflicted on myself. Like I chose wrong, even though it was the choice I had to make because I had no other choice to be with my family. I had to reclaim my choice and my options, and that meant going to a prison every weekend, where I had less choices about how I dressed, what time I got to spend with my husband, and how we made our family work. My favorite choice was when Jason and I chose to expand our family, and I had my resistance baby.

RESISTANCE BABY

I thought I was through learning. I'd figured out every prison, how to be a mom, how to get married, but I didn't know I still had to learn about my body. I thought I would never have any more children after Tre and Eamon. Especially after having Tre at fifteen and Eamon at eighteen. Being so young attached a lot of traumas to both pregnancies—the shame from others about being young, and the fear of what would happen to me and my babies. The shame and fear coming from my own family made it even worse. Being pregnant made me feel about as low about myself as I had ever been. As my children grew up, I thought that part of my life was done. I was not ready to be a pregnant lady again.

At twenty-eight I had it all figured out, and everything had finally fallen into place. Maybe not the way I thought. I had all my plans at fourteen, but life said, *Bitch, sit the fuck down. That's not happening.*

When I was fourteen the plan was:

- Graduate from high school
- Go to Spelman
- Go to med school to become an obstetrician
- Find my husband in college; he would be at Morehouse
- Marry at twenty-five
- Have two kids, a boy and a girl
- Nice house with the white picket fence

What I got instead was:

- Got pregnant in ninth grade
- Leave high school to go to an alternative school for pregnant girls/young moms
- Jason goes to prison right after Tre is born
- Graduate high school a year early
- Drop out of junior college after two semesters
- Start a job at a phone company
- Go back to school at twenty-five
- Get married (in a prison)

But either way I went, I still wound up with everything I wanted, more or less: graduated high school (and a year early at that), found a job I actually liked that was able to sustain my family, married my childhood sweetheart, had two kids who were doing well, was on track to graduate from Cal State, San Bernardino, joined the sorority Alpha Kappa Alpha, was a McNair Fellow on a direct path to graduate school, was on the dean's list, and just found out I was named the Outstanding Undergraduate of the College of Social and Behavioral Sciences. I felt light for the first time in a decade. I was finally satisfied.

And now I was ready to entertain growing my family like I never before thought I would. First, everything was going so well, and the big kids were big. My kids were almost grown, so I could handle one little kid. Second, I was *grown* grown. I didn't have to be scared of telling my mom anymore. Telling her I was pregnant the first two times had been a mess. And finally, I was ready to do this before Jason got home. I was in a position to navigate the prisons, I knew the routine at Ironwood, I figured out Calipat, I could figure out anything that came up. Jason only had eight more years left, so the baby would still be little when Jason got home, and I knew how to raise a family and navigate prison simultaneously. But most importantly, I knew that when Jason came home in eight years, he would be like a baby. I would have to teach him how everything worked and help him out readjusting to the free world. How to get a job. Anything tech. Cell phone. Microwave. Computers. Filling out an application. Getting an ID, Social Security. I wasn't about to raise two babies at the same time. So if we had a kid now, then the baby would be eight and big enough to handle himself, and Jason would be the thirty-eight-year-old baby I would have to help out.

Twenty years seemed like forever when I was fifteen, but now that I was twenty-eight, I had seen and done so much that I knew the next eight years of Jason's sentence were going to fly by. Prisons warp time and space. For me on the outside, I was always moving, so I didn't process how much time had passed until I looked at my kids. Jason had been inside for twelve years, but we saw each other almost every weekend and talked on the phone every single day, multiple times a day. We were good together. I was finally happy with my life, and I was ready to have my happiness on my terms. There was no more making decisions just for survival. Everything felt right. I was ready to have another baby, but intentionally and on my terms.

Jason had his own reasons for wanting to have another baby. He loved me; he loved Tre and Eamon. He wanted to grow our family. He also kept joking about how having another kid would make us attached forever. He always added a "haha," or a "just kidding," but I knew there was part of him that was serious about planting his little flag of toxic masculinity.

On one hand, he wanted a chance to start all over again and go through the infancy stage "together," since with the first baby, we were distant in our relationship and especially distant after he got locked up. Still, most of the burden was going to be on me again for raising this baby, but it was a chance to start fresh. He was scheduled for release in 2016, so if we had a baby around 2008, that meant there would still be a kid in the house, and we could be a family together—even though Tre and Eamon would be young adults. But the real piece was connection. Jason and I were already bonded for life with Tre. He was our first baby together; he was our connection. Eamon was not his biological son and was a source of real tension and anger for Jason early on in our relationship, but he came to love and adopt Eamon in every way except on paper. But a third baby, a second child that was biologically connected to me *and* Jason, would seal our connection forever. Every joking tone he used was a cover-up for the way he thought about me and us. Tre connected us, our marriage connected us, but a second baby would make me his property forever, but it was masked with "loving hard" or "just joking." At the end of the day, marriage is a piece of paper. Especially since we didn't live together and he was in prison. I could tell he thought a second baby that was both of ours would make it so I would never leave him. Instead of seeing the giant red flag as a warning, I thought it was love. He loved me so much and wanted to have a baby so badly, of course it was because he loved me. Silly as shit.

So we decided to have another baby.

● ● ●

As somebody who got pregnant the first time she had sex, I didn't understand how hard it would be to intentionally have a baby. Actually trying to have a baby is a whole different game. My mom had tried to scare me as a kid that "any time you have sex, you can get pregnant," which is technically true, and my mom was a nurse, so it had to be true. Look at Tre and Eamon. But once Jason and I decided to try and have a baby, I didn't realize that it wouldn't come easy.

When we tried to make a baby, I had to learn about my body in ways I had never been taught by anyone in my family. I learned that it's not innate for women to have a baby. I saw other women close to me go through fertility struggles for different reasons, and it opened my eyes to the lie that sex equals pregnancy. The lie that pregnancy is a birthright or guarantee for women.

At first I thought it would be easy. So we started trying on the family visits. I stopped my birth control. We had our family weekend visits where we could spend days together in the little duplex houses in Ironwood. I got to come on a family visit every five weeks, so I figured after our first couple of tries that would be it. But then nothing happened. I cried every month when my period came. What the fuck was going on? That's when I had to learn the human body, and my own body. I learned about ovulation and fertile days. At fourteen most kids are taking sex ed to learn how not to get pregnant. Me at fourteen was already pregnant from my first time having sex. Now here I was, a whole-ass adult, having to learn sex ed in order to get pregnant.

Months passed, and still no pregnancy. But I learned how to track my menstrual cycle so I could get pregnant. I started to schedule my family visits around my fertility. I stopped taking whatever was available, tracked my calendar, and asked for the weeks and days I needed to get pregnant. I worked the family visits around my calendar rather than the state's calendar or Jason's calendar. And once I made the visits about me and Jason, and stopped taking the first available spot, it happened. I was pregnant with my resistance baby.

The prison-industrial complex is based on an idea of punishment and control. Not singular, not just punishing the person—you're punishing their family, their community, anybody who is connected to them and loves them. Having a family, staying connected to a family, even growing a family, are not a part of the punishment scheme. But it is a part of the system of control. Add on that most people getting sent to prison are of childbearing age. At the time, the California Department of Corrections and Rehabilitation limited the number of contraceptives you could bring to a family visit. Seven condoms. So if you were *not* trying to have a family and if you were not trying to be on birth control, the state was controlling how many times you got to have sex on a family visit. Prisons aren't about starting a family, continuing a family, having a family. It's punishment and control of people, pure and simple.

So when me and Jason decided to have a baby, it wasn't just about growing our family or staying connected. It was about resistance. And not even in a concerted organizing strategy; at the very least, it was a big fuck-you to the prison, because we were taking back control of ourselves and our family. Prison invades so many parts of your life, it makes decisions for you. Whether to get married. Whether to have kids. How you get married. How you have kids. Prisons are always the third person in the relationship, but they take up all the space and all the power. Prisons make you ask questions you should never have to ask: *Do I give up the love of my life? Should I just settle for somebody else? Do I keep my kids in contact with their parent or just move on like they didn't exist? Do I even keep seeing the person I love?* Prisons do a lot of direct control over people inside and during visits: tell you where to go, how to move, how to act, how to dress, how long you can stay, what you can bring, how much money you can bring, what to eat. But all these rules about direct control are also about indirect control. It's not just about how to dress and what to eat; it's about making you question whether it's worth it to come to visit every week, every month, every year, ever. They're little burdens, little obstacles, little rules to make the whole visitation process feel burdensome and not worth the effort, until they make *you* feel worthless. People outside of prisons in the free world will stop going to a whole restaurant chain because of one bad experience at one location, drop their whole cell phone service because of one bad representative. *You* think all the hoops and hurdles aren't designed to make you quit? A big part of why mainline mamas show up every weekend, dressed to code, looking good, with a smile, not looking defeated or showing any signs of how much this shit crushes their soul a little bit each week, happy to see their family? Because they get to see the people they love and say fuck you to the state at the same time. That puts a smile on my face.

● ● ●

All of my work had to pay off. The planning. The tears. The back-and-forth of the arranged family visits and my cycle. Jason was the smallest part of the process, because it was really negotiating the back-and-forth with my real *man*: the state. My cycle. My schedule. All Jason had to do was show up. Trying to get pregnant was a full-time job. Plotting with the state. Anxiously waiting for my period to *not* show up after every visit. Six months of planning, trying, and failing.

One weekend after the three-and-a-half-hour drive from LA, Mo'nique and I got to the Motel 6 in Blythe. Drives out to Blythe weren't time for sad shit, for whatever was stressing you out. Drives meant Mo'nique's new playlist, the catch-up of the latest prison gossip, fun shit that happened during the week. Life was hard enough and our lives were different enough, but as much as the prison tried to take over our lives, our men and the sadness were not the center of the universe. On visit days we would barely see each other. Visit days were about the visit, so when we drove, we took the time to talk unfiltered and un-surveilled by our men, un-surveilled by the state.

So when we got to the room, we started to turn off our weekday self, calm down from the fun of the drive, and get to preparation for the visit. And that had to start with the room. If there was anything else available in Blythe, you know me and Mo'nique would be staying elsewhere. This was no luxury community. Motel 6 was fancy living for Blythe. So we had to strip those itchy-ass covers, wipe down the room, put our own comforters and covers that we brought from home on the beds. At home in the real world, we had real jobs and real places to stay. On the weekends we brought a little bit of home in our covers and comfort to this drive-through town. Somebody had our spot on the line for tomorrow; usually Mo'nique would either bring her own car or have it arranged that we would drop a car off. By now everybody knew who we were and what it was, so there were no problems getting ready for the line. But by the time we got the line figured out, the room set up, there was just enough time to grab something at Popeyes and kick it to watch TV. Sometimes, if we were lucky, there was a movie worth seeing at the movie theater, or maybe Mo'nique would go to the little casino she found in Lake Havasu, but never stay out late. We didn't sleep in like regular folks on the weekend; we got to be up early to get to the line. Tonight was an inside night, so we got our room, got it set up, got our food, and sat on our beds, trying to get comfortable, trying to find something to watch on TV.

Out of nowhere, Mo'nique said I looked pregnant. I started laughing hysterically. For a few seconds I had stopped looking at my tracker, stopped worrying about the pregnancy and the baby. Just when I had let my guard down. Everyone had been telling me it would happen the second I stopped trying and stopped thinking about getting pregnant. I had finally stopped thinking about being pregnant, and now Mo'nique was telling me I was pregnant. This was too simple. I had to go check my period calendar app. Lo and behold, I was one day late. My shit wasn't like clockwork, so I knew better than to get my hopes up. But the extra side of me said, *Bitch, we up.* But we were in Blythe. And we were in Blythe for the night. I wasn't about to drive thirty-plus minutes to find a CVS. Before I could say anything other than a laugh, Mo'nique jumped in. "C'mon, we're going to Dollar Tree; they got tests." I was confused. It's Dollar Tree. I thought Mo'nique was making shit up. I'd never seen a pregnancy test there, but even if they did have tests, it's Dollar Tree. The shit costs a dollar. You want me to spend one dollar and to trust this? It's fucking bootleg.

But there it was at Dollar Tree, in the last place I'd expect, the last test, right next to the register. Now time to pee on a stick in a Motel 6. I wanted to get food on the way back, but Mo'nique insisted we get back to the hotel and do the test first. She was more excited than me at this point. Then we waited for the longest three minutes. I didn't even leave the room; I was just sitting on the toilet, trying not to look at the test next to me on the counter. Mo'nique just kept harassing me through the door. "What it say? What it say?" And then two lines showed up. I was in business. My resistance baby was on the way.

Jason called me that night, and it took everything not to say anything to him. I wanted to tell him in person. Mo'nique was, of course, the first to know, but she was jumping off the couch like we just got drafted. Yelling, smiling, rubbing my lack of tummy. She was planning this child's entire life in one night. After we ate dinner I called Granny and told her the news, but as plainly and factually as I could. "I took a test from the Dollar Tree, and it says I'm pregnant." Granny's "mmm-hmmmmm" was the joyful tone of a checkmark of approval, a smile in sounds that dips down quick at the "mmm" and jumps to the heavens with the "hmmmmm." This wasn't the "mmm-hmmm" of disapproval, dropping like Granny's hopes and expectations the first time I got pregnant. This time it was different. I wanted to wait until I got home to take a real, digital test to tell my mom. Even though this was a different time and different place, the first two pregnancies were a tense and fucked-up time with my mom. Now my mom and I were really good. I had a good job; my relationship with my mom had finally healed. But I wasn't about to potentially open Pandora's box on accident. But this was so much news, and I was tired. So I took my butt to sleep. We worked, we drove, we had fun, we had happy news, but this was a long day, and there was a whole day of visitation tomorrow, and the line wasn't gonna wait for anybody or any good news.

Once I got through the line, the check-in, the metal detector, the guards, the halls, the rooms, and I found my regular table in the regular waiting room, I just had to wait for Jason to get brought out. I was a happy anxious. I had good news that I couldn't wait to share. Usually I had a whole routine. When I got to the prison, I would get the good stuff that Jason liked from the vending machines—the Big Az Chicken Sandwich or Burger that you microwave like at the gas station, some popcorn or chips, soda, and some wings. The wings was the thing to have, in a little microwave container, barbeque. Seven dollars for five wings. If you're standing behind somebody, and somebody got ten wings, you knew they had *money* money. Blythe turned me into a Starbucks queen; I would get my little cheese Danish, snacks, and coffee all eaten and taken care of before I got in line. I wasn't about to get wings out a vending machine and get bubble guts at a prison and use their bathroom. But this time I got right to business—no snacks, not even the wings—because I wanted to get straight to the visit. This time it was just me watching the window on the security door to see who was gonna come out.

I could already tell this pregnancy was changing me, because I had never been a door stalker or watcher in the whole time I had been visiting. I had my routine: I get the snacks, I wait patiently. But that day, as soon as I saw his face, I knew I had to walk over and meet him. At Ironwood they had a small, taped-off rectangle, about as wide as the doorframe, right to the edge of the allowed space. The prison painted a box around the door and entry area to keep people back, not about no safety keeping people from getting hit by a swinging door. The prison didn't want anybody seeing behind the door.

When they brought Jason out, I was there, waiting right behind the line. I was already turning into an extra girly girl, breaking my routine. I prided myself on not being thirsty. He would come out when they brought him out. I wasn't about to be like the thirsty girls circling the taped-off box like a vulture. But now, Dollar Tree said we were having this baby, and I was a new person. I got so happy, I forgot where I was.

When he came out out, I ran and jumped into his arms and whispered in his ear, "I'm pregnant." It was giving Whitney and Bobby. Over-the-top, too much, lovey-dovey, mushy mushy, my man, my man, my man. Jason smiled from ear to ear. We both got caught up and lost in the moment. We hugged and smiled and lost track of everything around us. For a good two minutes there was no prison, guards, or other people. We were home, thinking about what to tell people and when, in our own world and space. Jason could smile freely; we could hug and smile and just be. But only for a couple minutes.

We both realized we had to pull our happiness in. The rules say you get a brief hug and a kiss at the beginning and the end of a visit. The guards weren't trippin', because I had put in the work, talked them up, got to know them, to buy myself some leeway. Guards have the power to write sanctions, cancel visits, give us warnings, and embarrass us, but they wind up being a small part of the equation that is easy to maneuver. But people are always watching, and not just the guards. If someone else saw me and Jason hugging for too long and the guards not saying anything, it could create an image of special treatment and favors, and if someone took it personally and got jealous, that meant problems for Jason and problems for me. Prison pits all of us against one another; it can escalate some regular, everyday hating into real issues and real problems. Someone thinks that Jason and I have it good, might get mad, take out their frustrations on Jason, start a fight, then Jason gets written up, gets in trouble, visitation goes away. Perception brings issues.

This is what prison does to people. Visitation is a privilege, not a right. I should be grateful to the prison for these moments of happiness, the constant dangling of the carrot over our relationship. Any joy we might feel becomes part of the debt to the prison and the system. And any happiness comes at a cost. The roller-coaster abusive relationship with the state lets you know that you can't get too comfortable. Our moment of joy in making a baby that we can share only for a fleeting moment. We get a glimpse of the sun, but we can't bask. Prison eclipses joy. The whole world could be sunshine and rainbows, but the prison hangs over you like a gray cloud in a cartoon—just hanging over you, and only you. Every time things would be fine and joyful, the prison clouds would gather like a thick exhaust. Every doctor's appointment, every visit to the prison. People at school, people at work, people at the store, people in my family.

Once I became visibly pregnant, my relationship to Jason became real to people. Maybe they thought that our marriage was a novelty or some delusion I had about a relationship. People's assumptions about prison were just wild guesses from some patchwork of TV, movies, and urban legends. People just assumed sex and prison is either an orgy of men, secret behind-the-scenes sex, or maybe some kind of medical procedure Jason and I could definitely never afford. People couldn't imagine the little fake house where we got to spend our family-visit weekends when we got it. Even people who knew that Jason was in prison took my pregnant stomach as a license to ask wild questions. Even my own cousin, who had been to prison himself, had the nerve to ask me who I was pregnant by. As if they didn't understand Jason and I were married. As if they didn't understand the family visit. As if they couldn't understand that pregnancy is a thing that can happen when two people have sex. As if I hadn't been planning, and trying, and hoping for this pregnancy for months, for the first time in my life.

Sometimes people would ask it outright, but every question was some variation on "How?" It's one thing to ask somebody, "Who are you pregnant by?" or "Who's the father?" An invasive assumption on its own. People couldn't understand exactly *how* two people might have sex while one person is incarcerated. People wanted details and lost all self-awareness of *how* it made me feel, or *how* invasive the question was, or just *how* they were only asking because they were looking for some juicy, freaky escapade. A scandalous tryst. All the salacious details. They wanted a heist movie. Sneaking around a prison to have sex. Paying off guards. Hiding semen in secret containers. Some kinda drama. Rather than just some regular sex. The prison cloud followed me, but it got other people high off the fiction they made up in their own heads. Got them acting, and asking, and pushing, and probing in ways that they wouldn't have thought about if they hadn't been high off the proximity to the prison cloud. Pregnancy went from this moment of joy to months of constant, invasive questioning.

● ● ●

Prison is hard on the body. Pregnancy made it noticeable how hard prison had been on me. In my mind I was just doing ordinary things. Getting in the car. Driving. Sleeping in a hotel bed. But as my stomach grew and the pregnancy went on, it became very real. The drive got harder. I couldn't sleep in the hotel beds. And I sure as hell couldn't stand that vending machine food. The uncomfortable visitation seats became torture chairs. Jason and I talked through the whole pregnancy, and by the time I was six months pregnant, we decided that I wouldn't come for weekly visits anymore, but just for the monthly family visits. I'd come visit on those weekends, still with Mo'nique, but since I was going inside to stay, she would take my car to have in Blythe so she could run her little errands or go to the casino between visits. Mo'nique went from my mainline mama to my prison doula. She took care of business. She drove me out to the prison. She got me those cinnamon apple pies from Popeyes. She made sure I ate good, at the Sizzler or the Popeyes when we were in Blythe or by taking me out to eat when we were back home in the free world. When Jason got on my nerves, she was the one who would get on the phone and check him. Mo'nique became the core of my support system during the pregnancy.

This pregnancy was so different from my first two because my family was actually happy and supportive of me. The first two pregnancies, they didn't understand them at all and thought they understood my situation as a pregnant teenage girl, because they had been young and dealing with pregnancy too. But this time they were happy about the pregnancy, but the prison made no sense to them. They couldn't figure out what extra layers of stress and burdens and navigation I had to do. Even with my friends who had stood by me during my first two pregnancies and raising kids, the prison added something that they didn't get. More little comments like "You couldn't just wait till he got home?" Now that my friends were getting older and starting to have kids but weren't married, they all had something to say about my married pregnant ass because Jason was in prison. Me and my friends had stood by each other if people tried to say something or made them feel a type of way about their relationships or their struggles during the pregnancies. But because

Jason was in prison, it gave everybody a license to be slick at the mouth, less supportive, less protective.

Except for Mo'nique. She understood *both* the strain of pregnancy and the strain of navigating prison. Doulas support mothers as advocates. To make sure the pregnancy and the labor and the birth are about the mother. To stand up for the mother and support her against everybody. Mo'nique was my prison doula against everybody and the state. I wasn't the first pregnant woman she was close with. She understood how to deal with the system as a pregnant person. Everyone deserves a doula like Mo'nique.

● ● ●

So much of my pregnancy with Zion was different from my pregnancies with my first two kids. The sunshine and happiness of being married, pregnant, and welcoming this baby with the full support of my family. But of course the gray cloud of prison would sneak in, and seep in, and block some of that sunshine whenever it could. I did my best to keep it happy, and my doula and my mom all supported me. On paper everything was good this time, and there were no doubts.

Just when I thought I was grown and ready and supported and happy, the gray cloud of prison knocked me back to being fifteen again. Just me and my mom at the hospital for delivery. But the cloud wasn't enough to bring down this moment. This time Jason did actually call when I was in labor, but I was in too much pain to talk. Collect calls and labor pains don't mix. I had my own problems to deal with. This time my mom was actually happy with me. She was impatient. She wanted her little grandbaby. This would be everybody's redo and second chance. My mom was happy and wonderful with all the kids once they were born, but this was her redo during my pregnancy, through labor and delivery. She got to be her best self, happy, excited, and ready for the baby to arrive with joy.

●　●　●

After Zion was born I waited out six weeks in the house to avoid germs and exposure and give us some time to be together before I planned the first family visit. I wasn't working and traffic was easier during the week, so Tre stayed behind with my mom while baby Zion and I drove out to Blythe on a Tuesday morning. Got to be there by ten a.m., or the whole visit is a no. Family visits are already a trip through the prison when you're solo as a full adult. Then add a car seat. Diaper bag. Bag for me. Through the line. From the parking lot. Through security. By myself. No COs were going to help carry anything, and I couldn't do it in steps—what was I supposed to do, leave my baby in the car or with security? Everything had to be carried together all at once. I got real strong, just know that.

Babies had to follow rules too. Once you were in for family visitation, you were in for the duration. So you had to overprepare. A whole weekend of baby supplies packed into your bag. If you ran out of anything that you might need, there was no store you could get anything from. Visit over; you had to leave to take care of the baby. No going in and out. Formula, diapers, wipes, any supplies for the baby had to be brand-new and sealed. That was extra money, because anything you might have used even slightly before you got to the prison couldn't come with; everything had to stay in the car. And don't let you have any medicine for your baby. Any baby medications, like infant Tylenol, had to be of course sealed and new, but even then they had to stay at the front with security and couldn't come back into visitation.

Lucky for me, this was baby number three, so I had a really good idea of what I might need. Zion was six weeks old and breastfeeding, but I brought a can of formula just in case I was sleeping and Jason needed to feed the baby. A whole sealed, long pack of diapers with thirty-two newborn diapers. Even a thirty-two pack seemed risky for a weekend with a newborn baby. What if the baby got diarrhea, and we ran through these diapers? I almost brought two packs, but being prepared comes with costs too. I didn't want the COs to give me a hard time; you're only allowed so much stuff, so bringing extra means putting it back in the car or throwing it away. A thousand changes of clothes for the baby and receiving blankets. I didn't know how drafty it might be for him. And I didn't trust prison sheets for my baby. They put a crib in the family visit space, but I couldn't trust it. Baby lotion. Baby soap. Empty bottles for feeding. Clorox wipes to make sure everything was sanitized, because you can't trust a prison. A thousand nursing pads for me because you don't know how bad the leaking is going to be. And then all my clothes, my lotions, my usual stuff that I would bring.

Family visit turned me into Miss Sofia in *The Color Purple* when she was ready to leave Harpo; one woman carrying bags on bags on bags, and nobody even blinking an eye to come help. A car-seat carrier isn't light on its own; now you add a weekend of supplies for a baby and an adult. From the car to the security check-in. From the security check-in to the family-visit shack. No strollers allowed, because that would be too much like right. Nothing you can bring to assist you, not even an umbrella when it's raining. Any convenience that might make the visit easier is prohibited; only what is absolutely necessary in the eyes of the state is allowed—and even then in moderation. Because visitation is a privilege, not a right. "You can always not come." The state needs you to visit to keep people in line, to offer an incentive to the people the state has locked up, but the state turns around to punish you for coming to visit in the first place.

I hauled me, my baby, all these bags across the dry desert parking lot behind the cement walls of the prison. Even though it was January, it was still high seventies. I was sweating, my titties were sweating, postpartum, stumbling, trying to stay steady for the baby. No special parking for moms in a prison parking lot, just a hundred-yard desert trek across the asphalt. Then going through security, which thankfully was indoors. Just the COs going through everything. I knew all the rules, and I had an answer for everything. Everything was in code, and anything extra I had a doctor's note. I got allergy tested and brought my own sheets: doctor's note. Zion had to come out his seat so everything could go through the metal detector, and we had to walk through. Just like taking a trip through TSA, but we were going deeper into a prison. I was already going through security, and the COs couldn't tell otherwise, but I wasn't about to let anybody know how unprepared I really was.

After all the prepping and planning and learning about myself and my body for this baby, I wasn't really ready for what it was like bringing a baby into a prison. I had done it with Tre and Eamon when they were younger, but by the time I was visiting Jason for real, my kids were big enough to manage themselves a little more, and I didn't have to bring the level of supplies I now needed for baby Zion. And this was no regular visit; this was family visiting in our own little shack-space, so nobody was around to help me. Hauling from the car to security, from security to the chain-link fence surrounding the family-visit shack. I could see Jason peering from inside the front door of the shack; he wasn't allowed to move until the fence was opened, I was fully through, and the CO could lock the fence behind me. Finally, Jason could come out of the doorway and help me out. Once we had everything loaded in the house, Jason knew immediately to get my sheets out and put them on the bed, so I could lay my body down. I was tired. Meanwhile, Zion slept through the whole thing without a care in the world. He had been quiet the whole journey as I hauled him from the car through the prison. He was bundled in a blanket and covered to keep the sun out of his eyes. But when everything settled, then came the real treat: Jason pulled back the blanket and unveiled Zion for the first time.

Jason turned bright red and started weeping. This was Jason's first time seeing Zion outside the pictures I had mailed him a couple weeks earlier. Jason didn't say anything—just tears streaming down his red face. Like a wet cherry tomato. But just for a second, just enough to let out his joy, because he's no bitch-ass nigga. "Aww, look at you crying, little baby. Sensitive thug need a hug." Jason always had to act so hard, I had to bring the jokes whenever he showed his real, sensitive self. "You know I'm still that nigga though," he always replied. We started laughing and laughing as Jason tried to get Zion out of the car seat. If only Jason could figure it out. Prison is a time warp. Life moves on in the world, and in prison you get locked out of everything. These new car seats were designed for safety and theoretically user-friendly. But Jason had been in prison for almost fourteen years, since September of 1996. Jason had barely been involved in Tre's life in those first couple months; he wasn't taking Tre out of car seats or really caring for him. He was a teenager who got to visit under heavy supervision from my mom for a few hours at a time. Now Jason was a thirty-two-year-old teen parent and had to learn everything new. How to work a car seat. How to warm the water for a bottle. How to change a diaper. How to burp and feed Zion. I was roasting him the whole time, but Jason was learning.

Our whole dynamic started to change. During the pregnancy and even in the weeks after the baby was born, Jason didn't understand why I was so preoccupied or busy when he would call during the week. But now Jason could see with his own eyes that I was busy. This baby ate all the time. Woke up all the time. Had needs that could come up at any time. Our little family visit used to just be kickin' it, just us together, watching shows, enjoying each other's company. Sometimes Tre would be there, but he was getting older, with his own friends, and it got easier for everyone if he didn't come to every visit. That left time for me and Jason, which now became me, Jason, and Zion. Our family that we wanted and wanted and tried for was finally here. But babies, visitation, and life don't stay the same. We thought we knew what we wanted as a family, but we didn't understand what growing our family might mean for us collectively and individually. I didn't think about how much I would have to bring to the prison for visits, but that was something I could manage. It was real life that started pulling us away.

I started my master's program right around that first January visit. I got a new baby. Tre was heavy in his basketball bag, playing school and travel ball. I was running back and forth to court with Eamon's dad over custody and visitation. I had too much going on. All that every-weekend-coming-to-visit had to end. Graduate school took a different focus; it wasn't easy to finish homework on the weekend in the time between things. I had to read books and present at a level I had never seen. I had to learn how to be a graduate student. Everything was changing so quickly; there was no grace period or gradual adjustment. A regular family environment might have had room for trial and error, a family meeting to arrange a new schedule, or the sitcom sit-down to tell the kids about the new baby that was entering their lives. Instead, it was just me, on the fly, trying to plan around everybody, take care of me, Jason, the kids, and make decisions.

Changes brought out everything that was under the surface. As much as people want to act mature and understanding, people's real attitudes and behaviors pop out the surface. I thought I had learned and understood the masks that Jason wore, but I didn't realize how deep his problems went. His pride at my master's program, our new baby, how our family was coming together. But I didn't understand how miserable he was and how jealous he had become. Not jealous of other people in my life, but jealous of me and my freedom. As I started getting busy with Tre, and Zion, and school, Jason put his best face forward. "Don't worry about coming to the weekly visits, just come for the family visits." Jason was saying all the right things, but now there were too many right things. This was a script Jason had created of the "evolved gang member," not the mean teen gangbanger. I knew he put that face on for the COs, my family, anybody that he felt looked down on him. COs treat everybody like shit and my family never had a good opinion of Jason, so he had the whole performance down pat. He got his GED, telling my granny about going for his associate's and reading his Bible. I knew he put the mask on for everybody else; I didn't realize he was putting it on for me. I know Jason loved me very much; he wasn't manipulating me in the ways he was trying to play other people. But seeing me go on, grow up, have a life, graduate from high school, college, start my master's degree, have our baby, he saw a life he could have lived without prison, and he took it out on me. And I don't know if he actually realized it.

• • •

Jason started picking. Picking fights, picking at old wounds, start-ing arguments that we hadn't had since we were teenagers. Weekly visits turned to monthly family visits, but the daily phone calls turned to a gamble of whether it would be a good talk or an argu-ment. Jason started interrogating me. "Why didn't you answer the phone?" or "Why did it take so long to answer?" If I was out, it was "Who are you with?" If I was at school, "Why are you there so late?" I kept him up-to-date on every part of my life, so he knew the basics of my schedule and routine, so any shift in the day was a new series of questions. Not curiosity, just jealousy. Sometimes it would be in the tone or structure of the question. If I spent the day with a friend, it wasn't "What did y'all do?" It was "Why y'all been together all day?" Any background noise or voice was a land mine waiting to expose a potential insecurity. Waiting to catch me in some lie. For somebody from a dog-eat-dog world, everybody was on the come-up.

Our baby was supposed to be our chance to start over, but in-stead, it just reset our relationship back to the beginning. Jason's growth and conversations shifted back into Jmaek, the insecure teenage gangster. I saw hints of Jmaek peeking back out, but we locked into an emotional loop of spite and apologies, outbursts and then making up. I didn't think things would change nega-tively, because in all other ways, my life was getting better with my baby, and graduate school, and marriage. I had spent so much time in survival mode, on the fly, working to take care of the kids who depended on me. But with the birth of Zion, I started recog-nizing what I wanted and needed in my life and my relationships. I finally had time to slow down and think about what I wanted. I didn't know it then, but it was the beginning of the end of me and Jason. I was moving up, and Jason thought I was moving on. This was the beginning of the emotional abuse roller coaster. Happy love for weeks was just the windup for a huge drop-off of him saying something inappropriate, and us arguing, yelling, me crying, for weeks until he professed his love and how he was going to change, winding up in happy love for some more weeks before another drop. One minute I was in love and happy; the next he was yelling at me for not answering the phone. If he heard another man's voice in the background, he was yelling at me about how I was fucking that dude. All insecurities started bubbling up. He couldn't keep up as I was rising in my education, because he was in prison. So instead, he spent his time worrying about how I was going to find somebody better. Neither of us understood at the time that Jason had never dealt with all the trauma of his youth that had led to him winding up in prison in the first place. He didn't understand he was worthy of love, so his antagonism was testing my love. If he could make me cry, it would show I still cared. If I'd still show up to a visit after he done pissed me the fuck off on the phone that week, he would know I still loved him. Jason and I had a baby to resist the prison, because fuck the state, fuck everybody who thought we couldn't make it. We were defying the odds with our love, our marriage, and our resistance baby. I wasn't expecting my first baby—Tre, my day-one baby—to start giving me the resistance.

BOXED OUT

The mainline mama life is not for everyone, and as my kids got older, their visits got less joyful. When Tre was a kid, I'd take him twice a month—sometimes I just wanted to go by myself, and it's a lot for a kid to have to go through the line, the security, and the surveillance. The older he got, the whole visitation experience got to be more and more of a burden. He wasn't happy about losing his whole weekend to a visit—the long drive, the long wait, nights at a motel that didn't have all the channels he wanted to watch, a TV he had to share with me and Mo'nique. Add in the fact that Tre was getting older, becoming a teenager with friends, and a basketball talent at that. Weekend visits got harder because it meant choosing between basketball and spending the weekend at the prison.

Jason got moved again, from Ironwood to La Palma Correctional Center, a private prison in another state. Now, instead of the three hours to Blythe, it was six or seven hours to Eloy, Arizona. It was a tense time. I was having a struggle with Tre the teenager. I was finishing my master's degree and Tre was excelling at basketball, but that meant games and tournaments for Tre, both in school and travel ball. Tre and I started to get into it regularly, arguing over everything and nothing. I wasn't able to get out to visit every weekend between taking Tre to basketball and my money getting funnier and stretched out from paying for school, basketball, every little thing. Now I was making it out to visit less—it was farther away, and I didn't have a Chastity or a Mo'nique. That wasn't because of anything at the prison or the system.

Visiting La Palma was even easier than Calipatria or Ironwood because nobody was driving all the way out to Arizona to visit. Even though California started exporting everybody from the California state prisons out to Arizona private prisons. No big line, no big problems. It was back to the problems of High Desert—slow to check in, but so few people that it wasn't a big rush or strategy. Even the later visiting hours made life easier, but visitation in Arizona got hard. Jason was incarcerated by the state of California, he was treated like property of California, and California rules still applied. Arizona prisons didn't allow family visits like California, but because Jason was under the California Department of Corrections, now Arizona had to allow him and the other incarcerated folks from California family visits. So Arizona put in their least effort and let the family visits happen.

● ● ●

When I was in eighth grade, my algebra class got put outside because there was no more room. The classrooms were at capacity, and there was no extra space. Nobody was spending on building a new building, so the school built little classrooms sitting outside the main building. A little manufactured shack outside the back of the school. It felt like a shipping container. Cheap gray vinyl paneling. A thin layer of carpet. Tiny space. Built for temporary use but looking like it had been there forever. And don't let you find yourself in an earthquake in that little shack. Nothing for real to keep you safe.

Now here I was as a grown-ass adult, thirty-two years old and walking back up to my eighth-grade classroom for my family visit. Tre and I had come through visitation, processing, parking, everything like I expected and had gone through at High Desert, Calipatria, and Ironwood for years. For once Zion was the one staying home with my mom, and Tre came with me on the family visit—no special reason, just a shift from our usual routine of Tre with his grandma, Eamon with his dad, and me and Zion doing the family visit. Tre and I passed through the metal detector with no problem to go to the big beige metal door to exit the visitor processing center. A short cement walkway led to a fork in the road. To my immediate right, maybe twenty feet from the processing center, was a cheap chain-link fence surrounding my eighth-grade classroom—a little mobile home that has been there too long but looks like it got put up last night. To my immediate left was another big, heavy beige metal door, which led you to the main visitor's room.

Now Tre and I walked up to this cheap little temporary-yet-timelessly-busted unit out of my junior high school sitting right outside of visitation. A family visit is the only private time that you get with somebody who is incarcerated. But at La Palma, now we were in the middle of *The Truman Show*. Our family visit was on full display before everybody who came to visit. No yard, no private space, just some cheap curtains on cheap windows on a cheap little shack right across from the main visitor's center. But the loss of privacy wasn't just about feeling insecure, like you were being watched, or losing out on the intimacy that can come from getting away from the guards hovering around your table the whole time you talked. Now we had got potential problems for everybody. Jealousy from people inside and outside the prison. Arizona didn't allow family visits, so now everybody coming to visit was going to see the little shack for me, Tre, and Jason. We weren't giving up our family visits, and everybody should have had them. But not everybody got the family visit, so now I was worried about jealousy and problems.

I knew better than to stop when I was supposed to be walking in a prison, but I was pissed and in shock. One of our favorite things to do as a family during a visit was to sit outside. Even though we were behind fences at the little visitation houses in Calipatria or Ironwood, we could sit outside and enjoy the fresh air. Have little family water fights, but using the little plastic cups instead of water balloons to throw water. Summertime? In the desert? With some water? Nothing better. At least outside we could move around and see the sun. Tre always loved basketball, so some days Jason would ball up a bunch of toilet paper and wrap it up in a clear garbage bag they provided in the family-visit house to make a ball, and we would take the little waste bin outside, set it on top of whatever we could stack up, and shoot around like it was a real basketball hoop. But now at La Palma, everybody was watching. We were used to being watched by the guards, but we were not used to being watched by everybody else. The gaze of a guard was some relaxed Tom-and-Jerry game—trying to get the best of each other, be sneaky, catch anything. It was a game where you both knew the rules and the expectations. But other people on the yard were total unknowns. Maybe there were catcalls, comments, weird looks. Or just observations that got brought up in smart comments to me or Jason that pissed somebody off.

Tre and I hurried into the makeshift house for the weekend to meet Jason. I walked in and started venting. This was bootleg. Busted. Inside the room was the same setup I was used to, just packed into one big shipping container. The same worn and weird couch, TV stand, old-school TV, queen-size bed, four chairs around a table, a kitchen, but still no real cooking like Calipatria, only microwave meals like Ironwood. Jason and I decided to make the best of our time, but the room felt heavy. I was irritated and tired from the drive, and the visit, and the space. Jason was irritated with the space and with Tre. Not just because of today; this was a buildup of weeks and weeks of tension. Tre was fifteen years old and in his prime teenage attitude. He and Jason had been beefing over the phone for weeks. Jason had been yelling at Tre over the phone for not coming to visit more often, and trying to regulate Tre for being disrespectful to me. All Tre would have to do was breathe the wrong way, and it would set Jason off. I didn't even know what Tre said or how he said it, but with the first few words out of Tre's mouth, Jason lunged at him to snatch him up. My family visit turned into an episode of *Love & Hip Hop*. A casual conversation snapped and popped off into a full-blown fight in seconds. Now I was finally happy about this little sardine-can visiting house because I was able to go jump between them.

So when he snatched up Tre, I had to move quick. I knew what Jason was capable of. And even though Jason loved his son with all his heart, he was in a place where he couldn't show weakness or know his limits. I wanted Jason to chastise Tre and be on my side, because my fucked-up way of thinking was that Jason needed to confront Tre man-to-man and talk some sense into him. But what we had going on was a lot more than a couple of heart-to-hearts. Jason had snatched Tre by the front of his T-shirt, winding up with his other hand, so I immediately had to step between Jason and Tre and put myself in the middle before anything really popped off. Tre at this point was five foot six and damn near the same height as Jason at five foot seven, so they could still be staring each other down eye to eye right over my head as my little five-foot-three self stepped between them. But Tre was still a kid, and Jason was a grown-ass man from the streets, so Tre was starting to crouch and defend himself from Jason, and rolled up like a fucking roly-poly.

On the surface, my life was going smooth up to that point, with visitations, my kids, everything. But under the surface, tensions had been bubbling up with me and Tre, Tre and Jason, and even me and Jason. Our relationship had gotten even more strained since Jason got moved to Arizona. This was the last time Tre came to a family visit. The whole rest of the weekend was tense. Everything shifted. Tre and Jason barely spoke the whole time. No water fights. No garbage-can basketball. And definitely not talking about what happened when we walked in the door. The weekend was shorter and tenser than ever before. But this visit had brought everything to a head, and it was downhill for everything from there on out. Tre and Jason's relationship shifted entirely because they couldn't see beyond their own perceptions and imaginations. You couldn't tell Jason he didn't help raise these kids and was a presence in their lives even if he didn't live at home. Tre knew his dad, saw his dad, talked to his dad, but didn't consider him a real dad who was present in his life. It took almost a year for Tre to be willing to visit the prison again, but not on a family visit. Tre came once for a routine weekend visit after Jason pestered him into visiting. Jason felt totally justified in his actions and didn't think twice about what had happened. Tre was fifteen, which was an adult to Jason. At that age Jason had been in a gang, robbing people, selling dope, pulling guns on people. Me and Jason were strained from then on. Tre was at a transitional point of his life; trying to figure out who he was. Add on trying to reckon with the feelings with your father who you've grown up seeing on the weekends, who doesn't live with you, while dealing with Jason, who wanted to act like a parent who was around all the time but wasn't able to because of the prison.

Tre's basketball schedule didn't help. Basketball became Tre's first real love, and all he could see was the game. Tre and basketball at fifteen reminded me of me at fifteen with Jason. I didn't care what anybody else had to say; no other schedule or plan was going to get in the way of me doing what I wanted on my own terms. Tre and basketball were a little more structured, because it was such an involved sport. Not just with having to go to games and tournaments every weekend, but with the strong father-son culture of Tre's teams and travel ball, it made everything worse. Tre wasn't just playing for fun; he was playing year-round basketball for real. I could feel the boys' club at every game and every travel tournament. The coach would come and talk to the players, and then talk to the dads after the game. The coaches were polite and acknowledged me, but I could see the differences between me and the dads. There was kind acknowledgement, recognition, and appreciation that I was bringing Tre to the game, but if we ever talked basketball, there was always piles of mansplaining. Explaining to me that there were four quarters in a game. Telling me what "running suicides" meant. Talking to me like I was a precious old lady when I was younger than any of the dads sitting around, watching their sons. Wanting hugs instead of handshakes. Always looking at me like I was supposed to bring snacks. It was a very fucking rough time.

● ● ●

Tre's basketball schedule got more structured and became a huge part of my life. By 2010 we had moved up the hill, farther from the LA that I knew growing up. We had lived in Glendora, a suburb in the San Gabriel Valley that's still technically part of Los Angeles County, but definitely not part of *LA*. If traffic was acting right, which it almost never was, you could get from Glendora to LA in maybe thirty minutes. Up the hill in Hesperia and then Victorville, we were a good hour and a half away from LA through the Cajon Pass. People from LA stayed in LA or kept moving out to the suburbs for more space, a home, or whatever reason that pushed us farther from where we were from. We moved to Hesperia because my mom bought a house there in one of the new housing developments. Hesperia used to be a pass-through retirement community, a little town on the I-15 on the way to Las Vegas, but with nothing really going on in the town. At the time there wasn't even a Target or Walmart, just one movie theater, and a bunch of new residential areas popping up. Moving to Hesperia gave us a chance at owning a home with a yard, a space of our own. Basically living in Blythe, but at least we could still get back to LA when we wanted. If you wanted to go to a mall, a restaurant, or just get out the house and do some shopping, you had to spend at least twenty minutes going down the hill into the Inland Empire. When we were living in Glendora, Tre was falling in love with basketball, but it was all local—his junior high, some rec leagues, neighborhood ball that was all local. By the time we were

MAINLINE MAMA || 189

up the hill in Hesperia, Tre was moving into a high school up the hill, but now on a travel ball team down the hill.

Travel ball was Tre's love, and I was the third wheel. But Tre needed that wheel to get to all the practices down the hill and all the games in the LA area. So on top of the three kids, Jason, the prison, and my first year of graduate school was Tre's travel ball team. Practice was at least twice a week, plus clinics maybe twice a week, and then games on Saturday and/or Sunday. Every day had something to do with Tre and basketball. Zion got to stay with my mom, so practice and clinic were my time to support Tre. Practices I usually had class, but clinic I would park and come in and watch. I didn't want him feeling any type of way, and I wanted to make sure he knew I cared. My mom worked all the time and couldn't come to anything when I was his age. I understood why, but I also knew how it felt to be the only kid without a parent in the audience. So I went out of my way to show up where and when I could, like clinic and any games I could manage.

One day I was pulling up to park at the gym parking lot to drop Tre and one of his friends off at the basketball clinic at the gym, like usual getting my stuff together to get out of the car. Tre, out of nowhere, casually dropped, "Mom, you don't have to do all that; you don't have to come in if you don't want to." The way he said it was so conversational and insignificant, it wasn't an issue. I asked, "Are you sure?" He said, "Yeah," and went ahead in. For the next few clinics I waited in the parking lot for Tre while he was at the clinic, until Tre told me that his teammate's dad was going to drop them at home after clinic. It turned into a little arrangement: I would drop the two boys off at clinic, and the dad would bring them home.

I didn't think anything of it. Part of me thought this might be embarrassment. I was the only mom in the stands; he was a teenage boy. Maybe he didn't want more attention that his mom was the one there; maybe he didn't want me saying anything about where his dad actually was. But I took it at face value and tried to respect his wishes. At the time I didn't see that this teenage-boy embarrassment was concealing my baby giving me resistance. I didn't see the resentment; I just saw my day-one boy, who was growing up and figuring out his way in the world. I didn't see all the feelings he was feeling about his father—the hurt, anger, and abandonment sitting behind the toxic it-is-what-it-is nonchalance. He saw other people having an experience he wished he had.

On paper we were the full nuclear family. Me and his dad were married. He had two brothers who loved him completely. We talked about his day, we talked about basketball, we talked about school. Me and his dad had been together in some form for his whole life. But then you added in the prison, and his life was nothing like any of the other kids' that he could talk about. Tre saw his brother Eamon having a relationship with *his* dad, going to visit every weekend. Tre didn't know what a custody battle was, and the emotional toll it took for me to let Eamon go on the weekend, and the ways Eamon's dad pestered and harassed and badgered me regarding visitation and custody. Tre didn't know how Eamon's dad had physically, mentally, and emotionally abused me after Eamon was born. Tre didn't know that I had won a restraining order against Eamon's father when Eamon was young or that we had ongoing battles in court over child custody. I hid all that from Tre. All Tre heard from Eamon was that Eamon and his father got to go to Six Flags. Eamon and his father got to go to a restaurant and hang out. Tre heard all the fun little activities Eamon and his father would have together that Tre would never get with his own dad.

I tried to hide the realities of our life behind the on-paper representation of our family. Jason was in prison, there was no hiding that, but it made me work harder to keep up every possible appearance of connection. When you look good, nobody asks you questions. Maybe me and Jason couldn't take Tre to the store, but we could all look at the Eastbay catalogue and let Tre pick out whatever he wanted. Jason couldn't show up in person, but he showed up financially in ways that my friends' baby daddies didn't. Jason made an effort to send whatever money home he could, when he could. Maybe Jason couldn't take Tre to Six Flags, but I could make sure they talked every day, at least a hello. Some people don't even get that when their parents live in their house. I hid from Tre that between the hellos and check-ins were arguments with me and Jason, conflict, and struggle. I hid how much it took out of my life to take him to basketball, then go to school, then go to the prison, then spend some time with him and Zion and Eamon whenever I could.

• • •

Even when I thought I had things figured out and I could beat prison at its own game, prison still had the upper hand. Jason and I found a way to get married in spite of the prison. We found a way to stay together and keep our family together in spite of the prison. Jason and I had another baby in spite of and to spite the prison. But all this work in the face of the prison was covering up a lot of hurt and feelings that I didn't see or understand. I was going on my adult understanding of what family means and looks like, and not addressing the underlying shit going on with me, and Tre, and Jason—separately and together. I was so worried about the technicalities and checking the boxes that I wasn't dealing with the heart. I knew how to get through the red tape at the prison. I kept visiting and seeing Jason frequently and bringing Tre as often as I was able. We all talked on the phone every day. I told Jason about parent-teacher conferences, report cards, everything. I kept Jason informed on the surface of everything that was going on, because the surface was smooth, and that made conversations smooth. I thought if I made Jason feel like he wasn't gone, he wasn't really gone. We would be just like every other family if we talked on the phone, if I told him the comings and goings.

We weren't really talking, though. Just conversating. Not talking about what's in the heart. I didn't ask Tre if he was bothered going to basketball when I was the only mom there. I wasn't asking Tre how much he enjoyed going to visit the prison. I wasn't asking Jason how his heart was, or how he was doing for real. I wasn't asking the hard questions. I was still living as a single parent, still the human doing, oblivious and on autopilot. If somebody wasn't telling it to me, I was not thinking about it because I got a million other things on my plate. But I knew if I asked those questions, the smooth surface would show me what I knew was underneath. Pain and grief. Grief of what life was supposed to be, what could have been. I was supposed to be an ob-gyn Spelman alumna married to my Morehouse man behind my picket fence. I was trying to keep myself believing that my man behind the chain-link fence, my Cal State sociology degree, everything I had in my life now was the same as I imagined it. I still loved so much about my life, but I was pretending like everything turned out the way *I* wanted it to, instead of embracing that I was getting what I wanted in spite of everything that had happened around me. If I acknowledged everything, I knew everything might fall apart. I was so focused on keeping us together and saying fuck the state, I lost track of my heart, Tre's, and Jason's.

200 AND A BUS TICKET

Funny story. In all my years of visiting prison, I never debated just packing up and moving my life to a prison town. I saw how Chastity had it at Calipatria and how easy it was to visit. I thought that would be the life—easy visits, constant contact. But I wasn't about to take a downgrade in pay to live in a silly-ass little prison town. I'd rather drive every weekend from LA. But after High Desert, Calipatria, and Ironwood, Jason was now at La Palma in Eloy, Arizona, and I was about to move right next door. But not to visit. I got into a PhD program in justice studies at Arizona State University and was getting ready to move to Tempe, Arizona. The shortest distance between me and Jason since he had been on the streets. In Jason's wedding ring, I had "new chapter" inscribed on the inside. That was my signal that we were entering the new chapter of our lives together. We weren't teenagers anymore. We weren't just jumping into things for the fun of it. We were getting into a relationship, eyes open, knowing everything about each other. No more kids, no more sneaking around; we were declaring our love to the world. But it wasn't until I got to Arizona that the new chapter of my life really started.

Arizona was the first time in my whole three decades of living (at the time) that I was starting to worry about me. My priorities shifted for the first time, because I had put other people's feelings and needs in front of my own. I cared for people the way I wanted to be cared for. This was the first time I wasn't putting everyone else's feelings and stuff before handling my business. I started asking myself what I wanted, needed, and deserved. I wasn't putting all my time and energy into Jason and my kids. By the time I got to Arizona, I had been a mom longer than I hadn't. I was thirty-two and had been a mom since I was fifteen years old. That was the life I knew. But Arizona was also the first time I moved away. Every time I had moved before, I had moved maybe thirty minutes away from my mom or my granny. This was my first time in a different state, where I wasn't going to be just down the street from everybody else. I was living farther from my family than I had ever been, and I was living closer to Jason than I ever had. The driving distance was finally flipped.

Moving away from my family was no joke. I've always been an independent person, and I was confident in my ability to find everything in Arizona. But cutting ties with Jason was the hardest thing I would ever have to do. I went back and forth, and then, funnily and surprisingly, my family talked me back into our relationship. Nobody understood me and Jason when we were together or choosing to get married, but now my family was sticking up for Jason and trying to reason with me and talk me back into the relationship. But after I had my resistance baby, after Jason and I expanded our family, after Tre started playing travel ball and things started to get strained between me and Tre and Jason, even as the new baby was bringing all of us closer together, Jason and I grew apart. Ain't nothing worse than an insecure man scared of a bitch doing better. Jason's little comments and digs over the phone kept building, and he'd be mad at me when bad things happened to me. I tried to talk to him about my feelings, but I was getting just silence over the phone. He was listening, but his actions told me something different.

So I had started going to therapy to try and unpack all of my shit. I was reflecting and talking and listening to myself for the first time and starting to realize the kind of person I was with. Just because someone loves you doesn't mean they have your best interests in mind. It doesn't mean that they won't tear you down. Everybody assumed the prison would be the breaking point for me and Jason, so when we were near the end of his sentence, my family was trying to convince me to just ride it until the wheels fell off. Now that I had invested so much time into my and Jason's relationship, my family was trying to get me to settle and avoid a different kind of embarrassment. They had already put up a fight when I stayed with Jason and when we got married—they didn't get it, thought it was embarrassing, but now that they had come to accept our relationship and the prison between us, they were more embarrassed by the end of it all. If I didn't see it through, then I had put in that time for nothing, and the story they'd been telling themselves and others would fall apart. No more narrative about how I had stuck it out, or the bond that couldn't be broken, or that marriage was a lifetime commitment. But me and Jason getting married was my choice, and so was my decision to end it.

●　●　●

My whole life has been a wild ride, but I had never taken the time to talk to somebody outside my close circle of friends about any of it. It wasn't until I was sexually assaulted that I actually forced myself to go to therapy. Like never getting an oil change until you totaled your car. I avoided all the minor maintenance that would help me out and keep me going—talking to a therapist, which would make my life easier—until my life got too hard to manage on my own. I thought Jason was the only person I could talk to. I still can't talk to everyone about it, and I don't know if I ever will.

When it happened, distraught was an understatement for my feelings. I went to a friend's house and wept on the floor, told them about how I wanted to tell Jason because I thought he was my best friend. I was also worried about his health. What if the person who assaulted me gave me an STD or something that would be contagious? My friend told me, "Don't tell that nigga nothing." Not because of my privacy or my health, but the way she said it I knew it came from the culture of blame in my generation. I had seen it happen to girls in junior high: girl goes to a ditch party and drinks beers with a boy, maybe they get to fooling around, but then the dude's friends start crowding her and pressuring her and harassing her into running a train. But then the girl is a ho. Even if you know in your heart and mind and you take a real look at the situation, it's clear that this was pressure and assault, it's still blamed on the girl. No matter what happened in the situation, the woman got the blame. And part of me was part of that mindset and blamed myself. Maybe I had done something. Maybe I had let this guy assault me. I knew I hadn't, my mind knew, but my heart said I had to tell Jason, and he would tell me it would be okay, and I would feel better. I knew I had to tell him, because he was my best friend, and I could trust him.

The next time Jason called I told him. I told him through tears that I had been assaulted. I didn't give him all the details, but he was quiet and listened to what I said as I cried and told him the story. He let me finish talking and then said one of the cruelest things that anyone has ever said to me. I can't remember his exact words, only the clarity of his tone; a calm voice with hurt beneath it. Not hurt for me, but hurt for him. Jason said maybe we should just go ahead and separate. He said he couldn't get over the idea of somebody else penetrating me. He made it sound like I had cheated on him. He wasn't yelling or cussing me out like I had cheated. So some part understood that I had been assaulted. But the part of him that couldn't see me as a person but saw me as his marital property told me I had cheated, and that meant we needed to separate. The conversation was over, and he had to go. We hung up, and I just continued to cry.

That day I went to the doctor, got everything checked, but the depression had taken hold of me so bad that I had to go on disability. I started seeing a therapist, and they opened my eyes to how I was operating, my family dynamics, and how I had been taking care of my kids and Jason but never taking care of myself. I had become an adult so quickly, I wasn't paying attention to myself. I knew my life wasn't perfect, but nobody's is, and I thought that was just the way life was. I had spent so much time trying to prove my worth in the family and forming dependencies, I hadn't taken any time to focus on myself. I wasn't thinking about my childhood, my family, and my upbringing. I was just moving forward. I had done myself a disservice because I was taught that this is just what you do for family. To lay myself on the line for everyone else because I love them, even when they wouldn't do it for me. I had kept doing this my whole life, trying to get my family to realize how good I was so they would reciprocate to me and show me the love and care I showed them. Therapy gave me the tools to see all this for what it was—to see how it was taking away from me until I had nothing left. Therapy started me on my boundary journey. It gave me the glasses to start seeing the world a little more clearly, and let me start really seeing people and situations for what they were and treat them accordingly.

Jason and I never talked about the assault again; we never talked about the conversation. He didn't apologize for what he said or how he said it. I don't think he understood the impact of what he had done. But he apologized for not being more support-ive. And I accepted it then. I don't think he really got it. I gave him grace, and we moved on. The therapy had started me on a journey, but I wasn't ready to change up my whole way of moving. Talking to my therapist was one thing, but implementing what they said into my life was another. I had learned so much about myself, I was scared of the consequences of losing people who I genuinely loved. So Jason and I stuck together.

* * *

In the dim light of the gaudy red candles, I saw my whole family around the table of the Buca di Beppo. Me, my mom, my aunie, Kawai, my little cousin Ka'Nesha, my granny, Tre, Eamon, my friend Ariana, and my resistance baby, Zion, all seated around the table with checkered tablecloths. Walls covered with fake salami, netting, pictures of the pope, every possible stereotype of the Ital-ian American experience, and a few extra they made up just for decoration. This was our big upgrade from Olive Garden, and so

conveniently down the street from my master's program at Claremont. We rarely got to have a big family dinner, not like when
we were kids and we would have dinner at my granny's house on
the weekend. Everyone was grown and had lives. But tonight was
special. I had just graduated with my master's in women's studies
from Claremont Graduate University.

Tonight was my night, and everyone was here to celebrate me
with joy. I had just cut off my locs that I had been growing for
the past six years—I had been wearing my hair in locs since I was
nineteen, but I had cut them off and started a new set when I got
married to Jason in 2006. I had just started my new signature hair-
style: cut short, natural, but dyed platinum blonde. I had on a short
purple maxidress, tied at the side like a wrap, with fuchsia suede
Jessica Simpson wedges and big round clip-on earrings that looked
like gems, but blended with fuchsia purple colors. Ariana had
helped me pick out this outfit because she was the fashion queen.
I was doing better than all these hos with my master's degree, and
looking better than all these hos with the fashion look I was giving.
I was standing out with my looks, but we were just sitting down
to dinner after the tour through the kitchen that was part of the
Buca di Beppo experience. I was talking and chatting with everyone when Jason called for the first time that day.

Usually when Jason called, I would drop everything and step
outside to talk to him. That meant if I was out with my friends,
family, whoever, the present world got put on pause so I could go
on the phone and talk to Jason. My therapist had given me homework to try and stay present when I was with people. When I
picked up the phone to talk to Jason, he was gushing with praise—
"Congratulations! I'm so proud of you!"—appreciating me because
tonight was my night. We were having a nice quick conversation,

but I remembered my homework, and so I asked Jason to call me back because we were just sitting down to eat. I wanted to stay present with the people around me. Everything changed. Immediate attitude. "Why you can't stay on the phone now?" Baiting me to choose between my homework and my old routine. The people I was with or my man on the phone. It was never a discussion before; I always dropped everything for him to talk to him on the phone. This time I stuck to my guns and told him I would talk to him later because I was out at dinner with my family, celebrating my graduation. I politely and firmly told him to call me back later. Tonight was my night. Now he had an attitude. "All right then." And hung up.

When he hung up, even in the dim red candles, the lightbulb was over my head, and I realized. Even after everything I shared with him from therapy, even after all the years of work, and words, and marriage. Even after being honest with my feelings and sharing everything with him. He wasn't listening to nothing. He hadn't been hearing me. Everything was about him, and he couldn't even pretend for one day that tonight was my night. That's when I knew we were done. But this time for real. Any other time in my and Jason's whole relationship that I doubted that I wanted to stay together, I chalked it up to him having a hard time or something going on in his life, and somehow that would make it okay.

After I started going to therapy I suggested he try it out. I shared some of my thoughts and realizations and all the good things therapy was doing for me. I didn't share what the therapist was telling me about him, and the conversations me and the therapist had about my and Jason's relationship. It was easy for him to hear and talk about how therapy was helping me understand my family relationships. He wasn't ready for conversations about us. Even though he saw how much therapy was helping me, and he knew he could use it, he didn't think his problems were that deep. Therapy was something that he would do when he got home, not something he needed right then. Therapy and prison don't mix. Prison is not a space for working on yourself, no matter what nonsense people might shovel about self-discovery and rehabilitation. Feelings make you soft, weak, and vulnerable. There's no space for you to grapple with your feelings. There're not enough therapists in the free world, so there sure aren't enough in the prison. Therapy in prison is for addicts and sexual predators, not couples counseling and childhood trauma. Prison is a small, closed-in place. Telling your feelings and truths to anybody is creating a future problem, because you don't know who's gonna know your inner feelings and problems and use them against you. And then if people use your therapy against you, you have to set them straight, maybe get in a fight, maybe get more time.

And that made it so hard in all these situations. He definitely was having a hard time. He wasn't free. He was incarcerated. He was property of the state. He wasn't home with his family. He had years of unprocessed trauma. But now I realized that that didn't give him license to treat me like shit because he felt like shit. Two things can be true at the same time. I was never able to hold him accountable, and he was never able to hold himself accountable. Anything that looked like accountability was part of a manipulation, because I was something he was actually scared of losing. His attitude with everything was "Don't give a fuck; fuck the world." So any accountability he gave me was only enough to keep me around, not enough to spark genuine change. I finally saw it crystal clear on that day: just because he was miserable about everything that went wrong in his life, he was intent on making me miserable with him. Could it have turned out any other way? This is what prisons do.

• • •

I know prisons like a close relative. My husband, my father, my uncle, my cousin, my friends I grew up with. All had a relationship with prison, and my relationships with all of them were also relationships with prison too. Prison was always looming, intruding on my family and my relationships. Prison was doing the job it was designed to do. Tear down the individual who gets put inside, and tear down anyone connected to them. Not to break them apart or sever the connections but to exploit the ties between family and use the person who gets incarcerated as a link in the chain to pull whole families, communities, peoples, along with them. Prison isn't about killing a person; it's about using the close relationships people have to slowly poison everyone they may touch. Making them sicker, weaker, unfulfilled. Trying to kill people, sometimes all the way, sometimes slowly wearing them down.

I spent so much of my time fighting the prison by centering my man, it left people like me outside the conversation. Mainline mamas *maybe* maybe come up as this oblique "collateral damage" to the men locked up. The concern over men's well-being. Don't get me wrong, the shit is fucked up and the men inside need advocates. But somebody needs to speak up for us mainline mamas too. All the women I met along the way had some kind of illness emerge. And all of us were fairly young. But in my time dealing with the prison, all of us had some sickness pop up. I developed chronic stomach pain. I saw people with depression, fertility issues, high blood pressure, diabetes—all these sicknesses happening that can slowly kill people. Suddenly these things were just dropping into our laps as we visited the prison. Not because the prison had put some poison in our food or snuck into our houses in the middle of the night to poison us like an assassin. The system poisoned us by leaving us out. By pretending like we didn't exist while exploiting us. Because visitation was a privilege, not a right. We were just a privilege, but privilege can be poisonous too.

I realized with Jason that it was time to stop begging for a seat at the table, and time for mainline mamas to build our own shit like we have been building the whole time. I started to shift my own focus and energy. I had graduated from Cal State, San Bernardino, with a degree in sociology and went to graduate school thinking that I was going to focus my work and effort on Black girls and reproductive rights. I started student groups as an undergraduate and wrote about the state controlling women's bodies. I thought this was the only way to make a difference for women like me, to give girls the choices and power they deserved. I started working with Susan Burton and A New Way of Life, helping women after they got released from jail or prison. The same mainline mama skills I had built up navigating the prison system I turned to helping formerly incarcerated women navigate the free world.

Between helping the women on the outside and visiting Jason on the inside I started to notice more who was showing up and who wasn't. In the line in visitation for incarcerated men were me and a whole bunch of mainline mamas like me. Showing up to help, give support, see their family, keep it together, and do all the things that are important for people. But working with the women who just got out of prison, the only ones again showing up to help were other women, like Ms. Burton, all the folks in A New Way of Life, and me. More mainline mamas. I shifted my focus back to the people that showed up for me in the ways I showed up for them. I kept my work with A New Way of Life through my time in California, and when I moved to Arizona I kept working with

204 || KEEONNA HARRIS

incarcerated women and shifted my dissertation research from reproductive rights to the mothering that we engage in as mainline mamas. Mothering our incarcerated loved ones. Mothering one another. Mothering the state. Caring for everybody, and not spending enough time caring for ourselves. The years I spent visiting Jason, navigating the prison, have finally paid off in ways I never expected. I thought my purpose of visiting prison was to keep my family together. But my purpose is to serve, support, and provide a platform to the mainline mamas like me. When I serve others like me, I honor myself, the women in my family, and the women who are holding it down in the line, on the phone, at home, figuring out how to make things work. We find family and support in one another, even as we support our own families, whatever that might look like.

Folks that identify as women, especially Black and Brown women, are always on the mainline for men who get caught up by the prison. Any type of injustices that Black and Brown men face, we are doing the organizing, the rallying, and we are being left behind when men get locked up, then forced to care for the men while they're locked up and tend to their children (biological or not) and our communities. All while being exploited by the state to keep the peace and keep the incarcerated men from acting out, because visitation is a privilege, not a right. We are always the reason for the season.

Dear Keeonna,

Chiiiiiiiiiiiiiiiiiiiiiiiiiiiiiiile.

You made it. Everybody survived! But nobody survived.

We are alive and we are here, all of us. Granny just passed, but me (we [I]), the boys, Jason, my family. We all made it. But we hold so much shit.

All the sacrifice of yourself for people who wouldn't appreciate it. So much I've learned, but with so much fallout.

Nobody walks away from prison. There's always remnants. Scars. Tattoos. Jason got all his prison tattoos, but all your tattoos mark time in prison too. Jason's portrait on your back. Jason's name on your thigh. Your/my and Jason's initials behind our ear. "True love" on your wrist. Our relationships, with Jason and the prison, are embedded in those tattoos. The emotional scars run deeper than anything else.

Prison is a lie. Prison makes you lie. It makes you ashamed of who you are, who your family is, your relationship to them and to the prison. People knew I was married, but not that Jason was in prison. It puts a shame on you that does not belong to you at all. Prison is an illusion of safety. It creates an imaginary us-against-them. The biggest lie might be that you send somebody to prison, and they're going to come back somehow miraculously fixed. Prison doesn't keep anybody safe. Prison is a mirage; why else do you think there's so many in the desert? Prison is a projection so that people can see what they want to see, usually some kind of fear that plays on the imagination. You might drive by and see the signs, but the prison itself is far enough off the main road that people are blind to what's going on. Not close enough to see the person, to see the humanity of everyone they have trapped inside. Because if everyone saw the people, they might start to question what's going on. Prison plays on the most negative pieces of the imagination and deep-seated fears.

To the outside world, you look good. And when you look good, people don't ask questions. And when they ask questions, they're shook. "Your oldest son is twenty-eight?? How is that possible??" "Jason was in prison for how long?? And you stayed together?? And got married??" The perceptions of the PhD and the assumptions about the mainline mama keep people guessing and shook. People assume you're some magical Negro because you don't look crazy, your kids aren't locked up, and Jason got out of prison and now works a regular job. They don't know how deep the hurt goes, how fucked up everything became, and how much the prison became part of your identity. It stays with you, because you (we) know what it is like. Your personal and academic experience of worrying about your boys is no speculation; you know how this shit works for real—personally, systemically, intellectually, emotionally. This shit is deadly, and almost killed you. A couple times. Your mental health, your physical health, all took hits. But you are inexorable.

Today Jason is home. But it's not the home you both dreamed of when you got married in Calipatria. You bought a whole house for you and Jason to make a home in. Now neither of you lives there. Jason has been home for eight years, and only now are you getting to a place of mutual respect. He's finally done some work on himself; now that he's had some space away from the prison, he's recognizing a lot of his blind spots. Since you had your first baby, you've had to be a parent. You were raising yourself, raising Tre, Eamon, Zion, even Jason. And now Jason is finally starting to recognize how much work goes into parenting. And it took eight years after the twenty years of prison to even be able to have a regular conversation without some disrespect creeping in. These are the scars of prison. Not that Jason isn't responsible for his own actions, but prison's roots are so deep in your thoughts, actions, and behaviors, they take over. Like a parasite. You almost have to take yourself apart piece by piece to start over. And it's not just in Jason, it's in me/you/us too. The lesson you had to learn over and over again: as much as you were going to rock with Jason, that's the energy you should have been putting into you. Jason showed you how to really fuck with you heavy. Jason wouldn't have come home if it wasn't for you. It was a whole fucked-up situation, but it needed to be done. Everybody survived, but nobody survived.

As much as you might have wanted—or thought you did the most—to protect your kids, you had your own blind spots. Especially with Tre. You didn't see, or ask, what he wanted. You were so busy with life—taking care of the logistics, getting everybody from point A to point B, bills and big feelings—you thought what you were doing was what was best. But you didn't really have a conversation with Tre about it. You fell back into the same trap you were raised in. Parents do what they think is best and don't even mind what the kids might think, want, hope for, or dream about. And that's where you fucked up. When you look good, nobody asks questions. You made sure he looked good and smiled, and you didn't ask the questions that would have exposed the resentment. Resentment with Jason and the prison you might have guessed and sometimes seen. But not all the resentment with you (me [us]). When you finally started to see how much he was holding in, when he got old enough for you to stop and really listen, you got blown away. You thought you were close. You thought.

I wish I would have checked in more.

I wish that I had more conversations.

I took everything personal as a parent, but I didn't take the time to dive deeper.

I should have sent Tre to therapy too. To talk to somebody about the feelings he didn't/couldn't/wouldn't tell me about.

Tre has the face of his dad, but your heart. The same things you were looking for as a young person, he was looking for too. And I'll always be sorry for not being there in all the ways that you/we/he needed.

Keeonna, I'm proud of who you are, who we became. You've made the biggest transformation. All those scars and tattoos you picked up from the prison, you've turned into something beautiful. Therapy taught you that the emotional and mental and physical scars all have meaning. And you've learned how to make it all meaningful to you. You are the author and illustrator of your own story. You can make the life you want. You turned the scars and tattoos that you accumulated from prison into something else. Jason's face on your back got covered up and turned into a dragon and koi fish, your favorite of your many tattoos. It's the story of a fish swimming upstream, jumping over the waves, persevering until it transforms into a dragon. Nothing is getting in your fucking way. You covered up the script of Jason's name with a picture showing the stages of a butterfly's metamorphosis. Making something crazy into something beautiful. There are days you forget that your tattoos used to be something else.

You finally have everything you always wanted. An amazing partner who sees you. And not in that corny way that people like to say nowadays. But who really gets who you are at your core.

At your ugliest. At your weakest. Who has given you the space to tear yourself down and build yourself back up. And loved you through it. You've added two more family members together, and now there's five boys. Can you believe that shit?

You finished school and became a doctor, maybe not the ob-gyn you thought once upon a time. But you got your PhD, writing for and about yourself and the other mainline mamas you met and bonded with along the way. Now you're at a university, working on projects all to benefit mainline mamas. Learning how to write grants and create programs for women who have to navigate the carceral system, to make it easier for them to create their own communities. To give them the resources you wish you had had sooner. A space and place for us to get what we need until the prisons end. And they have to end.

Mainline mamas support one another. We spend so much time navigating the prison, figuring out the rules, on top of taking care of kids and partners and family in the prison and the free world. A mainline mama becomes a mother to her family, and especially her family who are locked up; a mother to her friends; a mother to other mainline mamas and their families; and even a mother to the state. Making visitation a privilege and not a right means that folks on the inside and outside of prisons have to follow all the rules and guidelines, and help keep that authority of the state together. If the prison doesn't have us mainline mamas, they lose a key way of keeping folks on the inside in line, with the hope and promise of connection hanging over their heads. But of course, mainline mamas are clever too. We know how to break the rules without breaking the rules. But for all the mothering and cleverness that we do, we need support. We create our networks of friends and regulars and other mainline mamas who we can trust with the secret lives we might live on the weekends at the prison. But the shame and burdens we face keep us from getting the resources we need. You found out how much therapy meant to figuring out your personal relationships, including relationships to the state and to yourself. And you know how hard it was to find those resources. It shouldn't take horrible, dramatic life events to get people the support they need. So now you build those support networks. You work to fix those disparities in physical and mental health, and create systems and programs and communities that will help other mainline mamas. Building connections for mainline mamas to communicate, even outside our little bubbles at each prison, and with professionals that have expertise in trauma-informed healthcare. Because for all the care work that mainline mamas do, we need care too.

Keeonna, you spent the whole time with Jason trying to help him find his way home so we could make our home together, with Tre, then Eamon, and then Zion too. You worked so hard to help everyone find a way home, you didn't even know your own address. Remember how we said our people would find us if we stayed still? And you did. You found the chosen family of mainline mamas that you still talk to after decades dealing with the prison and almost a decade not having to deal with the prison on the daily. You searched for a home, looking everywhere but in your own heart. You had to find your way back to yourself. After years of driving the freeways and ripping and running, you found your way back to you.

You are home.

Love,
Keeonna

ACKNOWLEDGMENTS

This book was not possible without the help of fifty-'leven-hundred people. It's my story, but it didn't just come from me. It was only possible because of the love and support from my people, my community, and my city.

First, thank you to Caits Meissner, formerly of PEN America and the Writing for Justice Fellowship in 2017. They were the first to recognize me and give me a shot as an author, to believe in my work and capability and present me to the world to tell my own story. Thank you to all the fellow members of the inaugural Writing for Justice cohort, especially Priscilla Ocen, Nadja Eisenberg-Guyot, and Mitchell S. Jackson, who have supported me since the moment we met. Thank you to Claire Schwartz for helping me work through the earliest versions of my book proposal. The cohort brought me to Jenn Baker, who pulled me aside at a PEN America event to tell me she loved the first story I wrote that would become the first chapter of this book.

Full circle of course, Jenn would be the one to acquire my book at Amistad Press. Thank you for doing so much editing and heavy lifting in the early stages of my book, and for your continued support throughout my whole journey. Thank you to my editor, Francesca Walker, for believing in this project, seeing my vision, offering thoughtful feedback and questions, and ensuring I got past the finish line. Thank you to Amistad and the many wonderful people involved in bringing this book to life. Thank you to Tracy Sherrod for believing in my work from the start, and for your continued support.

A special thank-you to Kiese Laymon, my favorite writer. Your book *Heavy: An American Memoir* meant so much to me in seeing my relationships to my mom and my boys, and so in true Keeonna fashion I just randomly reached out to let you know how much I appreciated the book and how I was feeling as a writer writing my memoir. Thank you, Kiese, for making me feel *real*; what I'm doing is not just some bullshit in my head—it's a real book.

It's because of Kiese that I met the most amazing agent in the world, PJ Mark, who has been not just my agent but a friend and Aries twin. I would not have been able to get through any of this shit without you. Thank you to PJ and the entire Janklow & Nesbit Associates!

For the people who have supported me since the beginning of my literary journey, all the iterations and stages of my story and storytelling, thank you for always showing up for me in any way that I needed: Saretta Morgan, Jacqueline Woodson, Natalie Diaz, Megan Comfort, Reuben Jonathan Miller.

Thank you to Tin House for my first writer's workshop, and double thank-you to Tin House for my first writing residency, and A.L. Major, my residency buddy. Thank you to Edith Wharton Writers-in-Residence and Baldwin For The Arts for providing amazing spaces to create. Thank you to Hedgebrook for the residency and making me feel at home in the Seattle area before I made it my home for real. Hedgebrook became a little family for me as a writer, and even more so when I got to work there as a chef. Thank you to Kimberly A.C. Wilson, Amber Flame, Cathy Bruemmer, and the rest of the Hedgebrook family. Thank you to Haymarket Books and the Mellon Foundation for making me an inaugural Writing Freedom Fellow.

To my family, extended family, friends, found family, and all the folks whom I have met and who have supported me in this journey in my life and making the book, thank you. Special shout-out to Barbra Chin, who is an amazing aunt and has shown up any time I needed her to watch the boys to work on the book. Thank you Jahman, who has become like a father to me and softened my heart in ways I still don't understand. You came into my life to help heal me physically and taught me to heal myself. Without that, this book would never have gotten done.

Thank you to all the mainline mamas, especially Chastity and Mo'nique, who mothered me and raised me to do this prison shit. Thank you for becoming my family. Special shout-out and thank-you to Anthony Herrod and Jay Jones, my brothers still behind the walls. And my niece Vanessa. Free them.

Thank you to the women who made me. My granny (Erma Randle), Granny Matthews, my mom (Bridgett Holmes, aka Black Gold), my aunie (Natalyn Randle), and my sister-cousins Kawai Matthews and Ka'Nesha Matthews. Granny, I wish you were here to see this. My foundation and my strength come from you. There are no words for how much I love you. You lived a life not really being able to talk your shit and tell your truths; I hope that you're proud of me and proud that I'm doing that for myself. Granny

Matthews, who is the true teacher of self-care: thank you for letting us be free as kids, and always encouraging us to be ourselves. To my mom, my number one girl: We been on a wild ride. The best parts of me come from you. All I ever wanted to do was make you proud, and I hope that I've done that.

Kawai, God did a big one with you. I questioned God a lot over the years, but one thing he did right was making you my sister-cousin. You have literally supported me since I was born. You have always been my number one supporter and protector of my heart. Ka'Nesha, whose smile always makes my day brighter. You make me want to be my best self, and a better woman.

To my firstborn, my day one, Tre. You are my first love. You have changed me in ways that I still can't describe or comprehend. Even though we've had ups and downs, and I'm sure I get on your nerves, you will always be at the forefront of my mind and heart. You're the reason behind why I do what I do. Eamon, my big baby, you have taught me resilience, perseverance, and how to advocate. My quietest child, but your heart is so big, I can feel your love even in your silence. Thank you for all the ways that you've loved me. Zion, my resistance baby, who gave me warmth and joy and brightened my world. You changed my outlook on life. I had accepted my life for what it was, but you made me believe in what is possible. To Xi, for just being Xi at all times. I am in awe of you and the way you have endured all your challenges. You are the best person. I am so proud of your growth and excited to see who you are going to be in the world. Jide, my *baby*. Thank you for loving me so strong all the time. You remind me so much of my younger self, I get to love my younger self all over again every day. Hugs.

Last but definitely not least, thank you to Jeremiah Chin, who has been not just an amazing partner and father but an amazing human being. You have loved me through my journey, through sickness and depression; I don't even have the words to say how thankful I am that you are in my life. My only hope is that you feel that and that I do the same for you.

ABOUT THE AUTHOR

Keeonna Harris is a writer, storyteller, mother of five, prison aboli-
tionist, activist, and academic, born and raised in Watts and other
parts of South Central Los Angeles. Her work focuses on health
disparities and radical organizing for women connected to systems
of mass incarceration, mothering, and community building as acts
of radical defiance against carceral institutions.

Harris has received several honors including a 2018–2019 PEN
America Writing for Justice Fellowship, a 2021 Tin House Summer
Residency, a 2023 Baldwin For The Arts Residency, and a 2023
Hedgebrook Fellowship as the 2023 Edith Wharton Writer-in-
Residence. She is a 2024 Haymarket Writing Freedom Fellow
and a postdoctoral scholar at the University of Washington in the
Department of Health Systems and Population Health. She is de-
veloping the Borderland Project, a mental health and community
support system for women forced to navigate carceral institutions
to maintain connections with incarcerated persons. She lives in
Seattle.